Praise for *Lead with Influence*

Lead with Influence is an invaluable guide that provides keys to garnering commitment from others and outlines effective strategies to influence individuals in transitioning from tactical needs to fostering a strategic partnership.

—Deena Ghazarian, CEO, Austere

Lead with Influence provided our technology leaders with actionable, relevant skills to drive more value across the enterprise. The learning approach was structured in an engaging and interactive way, plus the facilitator's coaching made all the difference.

—Rahoul Ghose, Chief Information Officer, ECMC

Lead with Influence provides helpful and practical strategies that leaders can use to improve communication and build trust with key stakeholders enabling a deeper focus on meeting the needs of consumers and quality of care.

—Todd Gustin, CEO Genoa Healthcare

The FMH Marketing team was able to gain valuable insights from the Lead with Influence training they received and able to deploy these new skills right away. Since the course, the team has been able to continue building stronger collaborative internal relationships and more effectively position FMH as a consultive partner with our external stakeholders.

—Dave DeCapp, Sr. Vice President,
Marketing, Farmers Mutual Hail

The Lead with Influence program has been super appropriate for what we've needed to help our leaders develop both hard and soft skills as our business has grown rapidly.

—Jim Glomstad, CEO, Sportech

Lead with Influence offers excellent strategies to help anyone gain cooperation and support for their ideas. The concepts are very relevant in APAC and build upon proven Dale Carnegie principles.

—Hei, Yu Lung 黑幼龍, Founder of Chinese Dale Carnegie Training

Our directors talk about how relevant Lead with Influence has been for them. So much so that they've asked, "Did you somehow schedule this training today specifically for me?" You've nailed it in meeting them where they are.

—Anthony Hoang, Chief Technology Officer, CleanChoice Energy

Dale Carnegie's Lead with Influence teaches invaluable leadership insights by giving strategic guidance with practical application. Under the facilitator's expert guidance, our people have advanced their careers with newfound confidence and impact. Highly recommend!

—Gary Bridgewater, CEO, Baker Group

Leaders across our organization have found the Lead with Influence playbook extremely applicable as they enhance their skills to influence across the company, build more strategic relationships with key stakeholders and ultimately, achieve our goals.

—Lisa West, Talent & Leadership Development,
Securian Financial Group

Dale Carnegie

LEAD WITH INFLUENCE

A Proven Process to Lead without Authority

MATT NORMAN

Disclaimer

The views or opinions expressed herein are my own and reflect my experiences, reading, and research. They do not necessarily reflect the views or opinions of any individuals, institutions, or organizations I may be associated with.   —Matt Norman

Published 2024 by Gildan Media LLC
aka G&D Media
www.GandDmedia.com

Front cover design by David Rheinhardt of Pyrographx

Interior design by Meghan Day Healey of Story Horse, LLC.

Library of Congress Cataloging-in-Publication Data is available upon request

ISBN: 978-1-7225-0682-7

10 9 8 7 6 5 4 3 2 1

Contents

PART THREE
Propose: Making Your Ideas Known

PART FOUR
Persuade: Managing Resistance and Tension

PART FIVE
Institutionalizing Leadership Influence

. . . .

*If it's easy, it's probably
not worth doing.*

. . . .

Sell, Don't Tell

Clara excitedly waited for John to arrive at the coffee shop, where she sat sipping her latte. She'd long held John in high regard for his leadership and strong network of relationships. He seemed like a wise sage who commanded respect and admiration from everyone.

She wanted to do something more meaningful in her career and, if John was leading it, it probably would have an impact.

Eventually, John walked in and warmly greeted her. It didn't take long for them to get down to business. John had an idea and wondered if Clara would be involved.

Agrifood Energy and Bioscience, the organization where John presided as executive chairman, had an opportunity to start a new line of business that could make a significant mark on the industry and community. John laid it out like this:

"Clara, there's a huge opportunity for partnership around clean energy investment in our region. The government has passed a bill to fund new projects, and the economics of wind and solar has improved substantially.

"The challenge is that many renewable energy and technology companies don't have a strong history of collaboration with government partners. I think the power and money of our clients could help provide the needed incentive and resources to realize the possibilities in clean energy in our region. This would also be a great investment and opportunity to gain visibility for our clients. What do you think?"

Clara wanted to burst with excitement. Make an impact on the environment? Work on a project with John? Leverage her background in environmental sciences and investment? Work directly with top Agrifood customers?

"I don't need to think about it. Yes! I love the idea; it hits on so many things I've been dreaming about."

"OK, great," said John "I'll put together an offer letter for you to review. Let's set up a weekly call where we can talk strategy, progress, and needs.

"Just one thing. Tim, our CEO, is excited about this concept, as is the rest of the executive team. That said, I'd prefer not to distract them from their strategic plan. We have a huge opportunity within the existing market and customer base, and they are spread very thin. They'll support what you're doing, though it will be best to run a parallel path and keep them informed. How does that sound?"

"You got it!"

Although Clara responded with enthusiasm, something inside her had a flash of concern about running a parallel path to the rest of the business. "Won't I need their full support for this effort?" she wondered.

Nonetheless, Clara put her full effort into the work. For years, she'd been able to do the work of two or three people by herself, and John loved to see the progress she was able to make in just a few weeks.

One of the first ideas she set out to implement was to convene the top Agrifood customers, along with key energy, technology and government leaders, for an open forum about investment opportunities. She sat down in front of her computer and began creating a plan with work streams:

1. Event Planning
   a. Goal: Host an inspiring event that attracts top players and clients, leading to follow-up meetings to discuss fundraising and collaboration.
   b. Next step: select event planner, location, and date.

2. Branding/PR
   a. Goal: Establish a "brand" for this initiative with a landing page and basic marketing pieces.
   b. Next step: identify a digital marketing/design contractor to help with images, web page, and concept pieces.

3. Stakeholder Development
   a. Goal: Form key public and private relationships that drive opportunities for collaboration and investment.
   b. Next step: create target list of public/private partners along with background and contact information.

4. Environmental Review
   a. Goal: Understand regulatory, market, and geographic landscape for investment opportunities.
   b. Next steps: conduct due diligence and prepare environmental review summary report.

Clara had just started thinking about how urgently these next steps needed to happen to meet John's expectations when her phone lit up with a text from her son, Leif: "Mom, I feel really sick. Can you please get me at school?"

She wondered whether her husband would be available to do the pickup, but remembered that he was picking up their daughter, Greta, this afternoon for her volleyball game an hour away.

"How am I going to get all this done? I'm sure John will understand that I have a sick kid, another one at a volleyball tournament, and two more needing dinner!"

She closed her laptop and ran out the door.

The next morning Clara felt a bit sick herself, but she knew that she had to pull it together to join Agrifood's executive team weekly meeting. On John's request, Tim had added her to the agenda to provide an overview of the initiative.

Clara frantically got the kids out the door, including Leif, after giving him some medicine to reduce his fever, and ran up to her desk to jump on the virtual meeting.

She had gotten pretty comfortable with virtual executive meetings from her time in private equity. She would often join board meetings for their portfolio companies around the world. Speaking up, even with high-level executives in the meeting, was generally not an issue for her. She just needed to calm herself down, because she wished she'd had more time and capacity to prepare for this conversation.

After initial pleasantries, Tim opened the conversation with a reference to Clara: "Everyone please welcome Clara Daniels. She's a friend of John's and will be working directly with him on investment opportunities in clean energy that are derivatives from our core business. Clara, we're glad to have you."

"Thank you, Tim and team," she began. "I'm very excited to be with you all. Congratulations on your continued growth. As you may know, the market and regulatory environment is very favorable for investment in renewable energy in the geographies in which we operate. We think this will be good for our community and provide an investment platform for Agrifood customers—primarily pensions and venture-backed portfolios looking to diversify their funding sources.

"I'm organizing an event to socialize this concept in September, and I'd love it if you could promote it with your customers and consider attending personally. I realize you've got your hands full with the current business, but your support is appreciated. At this point, I'd open it up for any questions."

Immediately, a president of one of the Agrifood divisions unmuted herself and asked, "How are you planning to communicate to our customers? My only concern is that we've been sending too many communications, and we don't want to overwhelm them."

After Clara responded, another question came from the head of marketing: "Clara, great work here. Can I send you our marketing guidelines to make sure that anything you're showing or sending conforms to our brand requirements?"

For over fifteen minutes, Clara graciously responded to questions. She noticed a private comment from Tim come through the meeting chat: "Thanks for all your work on this, Clara. We're excited for the event. Need to move to our next agenda item."

That was it. Clara left the meeting and sat there looking at the screen with a strange combination of anticipation and fear. "Can I do all this?" she wondered.

That's when her cell phone started buzzing. It was John.

"Hi, John!"

"Clara, great work in that meeting. I know I said we should run this on a parallel path, but I'm realizing that we're going to need some things from the Agrifood leaders, especially their support communicating to their customers."

"Definitely. I don't think I can pull this off without their help."

"You'll need sales, marketing, and IT to give you some time in the weeks ahead for us to stay on schedule. Why don't you reach out to schedule a follow-up meeting with some of the key leaders? I'll send you a short list of those I think you'll want to get buy-in and support from."

That night, after the kids were in bed, Clara opened up her laptop and began drafting messages to Agrifood sales, marketing, and technology executives. She started with Leon Tripani, senior vice president of sales for the Agrifood bioengineering business:

Hello Leon,

I got your contact information from John MacLennan. He suggested I reach out to you to discuss an event that I'm planning for an initiative that John and I are working on.

The event will take place this fall and will feature many well-regarded speakers representing government and for-profit innovation in renewable energy. It will likely be around 11 a.m. to 2 p.m., so will include lunch.

I'd love to talk with you about getting a communication out to your larger customers inviting them to this event.

Please let me know your thoughts on this.

Thanks so much,

Clara

After a week, she had only gotten a response from the chief information officer (CIO). No one else had responded, which perhaps wasn't surprising, since the company was in growth mode. The CIO had written back copying his director of information technology (IT), asking that she see how she might help Clara with setting up a landing page and a database for collecting registrations and feedback.

Even after Clara sent emails to the others checking in on whether they had thoughts about her request, nothing came back to her.

Frustrated, Clara sent an email to John: "If people won't even respond to me, I'm not sure how we can get access to Agrifood customers, which is a showstopper. I get that they are busy, but at least they could grant me the courtesy to respond!"

Clara felt her anxiety and fear increasing as she contemplated how much she'd feel like a failure and how sad she'd be if this effort didn't gain traction.

Moments later, Clara's phone buzzed and she saw "John Mac" on the screen.

"Hi, John. Thanks for calling. Sorry—I'm just frustrated."

"Totally get it, Clara. I've been there," sympathized John. "What would you think about working with someone I trust to help you with your communications with key stakeholders? I realize you're a very accomplished professional with lots of experience, but I've found that there is an art and science to communicating with influence when you can't just tell people what to do.

"I've worked with someone who coaches leaders to incorporate the psychology of leading with influence into their mindset and communication when working with others who may be distracted, opposed, or simply have competing priorities. He's helped me and other leaders improve how we communicate so that we can drive change and achieve better results.

"I know you're busy, but this investment of time on your part may result in more velocity in getting things done through others. What do you think? Would you be open to meeting him?"

"I'm a bit skeptical, and I've worked with coaches before," Clara replied, "but I'm willing to have a conversation with him if it helps me speed up this process."

"You got it, Clara. I'll have him reach out to you tomorrow."

Collaborative Leadership and Influence

Like Clara, you and I have a choice about how we will attempt to lead others toward positive change. We can choose to influence with:

Power. We might have positional authority, negotiating leverage, financial strength, or some other source of superior strength. This can be helpful for advancing certain objectives but usually doesn't inspire trust, develop a relationship, or cause everyone to feel valued.

Expertise/intelligence. We may be the smartest one in the room or have more and better arguments for our cause. This too can lead others to feel inferior or frustrated and often leads us to being prideful and closed-minded to alternatives.

Hard work. We can "outeffort" people. Sometimes simply getting more done and outpacing others gives us the superiority in decisions. The drawback: the effort is often unsustainable on our part and prompts others to keep giving us more work.

Coercion. We can attempt some form of manipulation by mentally, emotionally, or physically forcing someone into compliance. Out of fear or pain avoidance, they acquiesce.

Passion and persistence. We can press and request until we get our way. The squeaky wheel gets the grease, as they say. Children learn quickly that enough whining and trying often ends up getting them what they want. But pressure makes us look desperate and annoys others.

Collaboration. We can influence others by engaging them in a shared vision and commitment. We can help them see the value of change and agree to next steps together. This form of influence creates the most lasting trust, because decisions have been forged together, with diverse input and consideration. Choices have been freely made, because people believe they make the most sense for themselves and others.

Each form of influence has disadvantages, and each might be appropriate in different situations. In this book, we will consider how to lead and influence through collaboration.

The drawback to this approach is that it comes with the risk that others won't reciprocate. It does take two to tango, and it takes a bit more of an up-front investment of time. But if you can find or develop a willing partner, you'll find over and over again that it's worth doing the dance, because collaborative influence builds trust, engagement, and commitment.

Influence without Authority

Uncertainty is where new value is created.
—KEITH FERRAZZI, *Leading without Authority*

Early in my career, I had to get work done with and through a talented and well-regarded engineer who built the technology backbone of our company. He knew everything about our systems and the company's politics. Being less than one year into my role at the company, I knew I had to be strategic if he was going to help me.

I tried to sound smart. I tried to be nice. I tried to be excited, to get him excited. I tried to rush, thinking that a fire drill might fire him up to my cause. I tried being deferential. He was nice enough in return, but he always acted as if I was interrupting and annoying him. His attention was in many places, and I struggled mightily to get it.

Whose attention or help do you struggle to get?

There may be several reasons you sometimes struggle to get the attention of others. One likely reason is that you're *telling* people your ideas and requests rather than *selling* them on your shared wants and needs.

To Tell or to Sell?

In 2004, I took a role in sales. Having been a technology and product person up to that point in my career, I had assumed from the customer meetings I'd attended that top salespeople were great because of personality and hard work (along with some luck).

Not fully satisfied with those initial assumptions, I pored over sales research and literature. What I discovered surprised and delighted me: *sales interactions follow a predictable flow based on the psychology of influence.* Said another way, if you're selling a prospective customer on your products and services, selling your child on the value of doing their schoolwork, or selling your colleagues on the value of a company initiative, you'll enjoy greater success if you structure your communication according to a psychologically researched process.

This became clear to me as I read about the Huthwaite Corporation's study of 40,000 professionals over twelve years, which revealed predictable patterns of influence. It was illuminated for me as I devoured Dale Carnegie Training's sales program, which laid out the proven psychology of influence. As I applied these steps to my communication, I ended up with much better results. In fact, I quickly rose to become one of the top performing salespeople in our company, even though I was younger and less experienced than most of my customers and peers.

Perhaps what attracted me to a proven communication pattern was that I *needed* a method to follow. Like King George VI, whose speech impediment was powerfully depicted in the book and film *The King's Speech*, I too have faced insecurities and limitations in my communication ability. As I wrote about in my book *Four Patterns of Healthy People*, I experienced major panic attacks while public speaking early in my career. And I lean toward introversion, so selling something over a round of golf or a fancy dinner made me tired just thinking about it.

Beyond those limitations and insecurities, my technical background helped me to understand the value of following a mental model. As my early work in tech and product moved to the more creative areas of design and user interface, it was clear that to be creative, you need a process. As the world-famous cellist Yo-Yo Ma has explained, there is freedom in structure.

This structure is not the exclusive domain of sales. It applies to any idea or concept you need to "sell," whether someone has to pay for it or not. It could be selling your reputation, selling a recommendation, or selling someone on why they should come with you to a show. As Daniel Pink says in his book *To Sell Is Human*, we all need to move others—especially if we want to lead with influence.

Because many people struggle to consider themselves salespeople or aspire to improve their sales ability, I'll use the word *influence* rather than *sell*. As the great author, speaker, and coach John Maxwell explains in *The 21 Irrefutable Laws of Leadership*, "The true measure of leadership is influence—nothing more, nothing less." As I often tell my kids as they leave for school in the morning: *form the culture around you more than being formed by it.*

Influence, in the sense that I will use here, is different from power-based techniques such as incentives, mental tricks, coercion, manipulation, or control. To better understand these, I recommend reading the Renaissance political philosopher Niccolò Machiavelli or Robert Cialdini's best-selling book *Influence*. Both are fascinating and sometimes helpful, but they are better suited to creating an employee compensation plan or public policy than to the leadership of a parent talking with their child about making good choices or the type of influence exhibited in a one-on-one conversation between a manager and team member.

Embrace a Growth Mindset

The other key to success for anyone seeking to increase their influence is to embrace a growth mindset.

Carol Dweck and her research team at Stanford University have found that in respect to change, people tend to have either a *fixed* or a *growth* mindset. As she explains in her book *Mindset*, a fixed mindset approaches change as something to be avoided because you've established and seek to prove your fixed ability: "I'm too busy. I know how to do this already. I suck at this. I hate doing that."

By contrast, a growth mindset characterizes those who view themselves as works in progress. A growth mindset operates on the "not yet" philosophy: "I'm not good at this yet. I haven't reached my potential yet. I'm uncomfortable, yet I'm getting better."

Not surprisingly, Dweck and her team have found that people with a growth mindset outperform those with a fixed mindset.

Nonetheless, even though most people intuitively understand that growth is better than being fixed, they avoid opportunities to change how they communicate. It's uncomfortable, it takes time, it feels awkward, and you might just be good enough to get by.

In his book *Peak*, the late performance researcher K. Anders Ericsson explains that performance improvement comes through deliberate practice, which requires:

• Pushing beyond your comfort zone
• Working toward well-defined specific goals
• Focusing intently on practice activities
• Getting high-quality feedback
• Developing a mental model of expertise

To get the most out of this book, embrace a growth mindset that pushes you outside your comfort zone. Resist the temptation to dismiss the ideas by saying things like "That's not going to work in my circumstances," or "I've tried that, and it didn't work," or "I do that already."

Establish a well-defined goal for your influence. Is it a promotion? A new company initiative? A seat at the planning table? Consider your world of stakeholders—people and groups who have a stake in your success. What breakthrough are you seeking with one or more of them?

Consider how you might practice the concepts in this book. Find a practice partner, form a book club, work with a coach, take a training program, record yourself, or whatever will help you try these strategies over and over again. Hold yourself accountable, as the famous "Miracle on Ice" hockey coach Herb Brooks of the 1980 gold-medal winning U.S. men's hockey team did with his team when he made them practice "again, again, again, and again."

As you're practicing, make sure to get high-quality feedback. As Ericsson explains, it's not that helpful to whack away at a bucket of golf balls at the driving range unless you're tracking which adjustments are leading to which outcomes and trying to replicate the adjustments that yield the best outcomes.

Finally, lock in a mental model of expertise. Get to a place where you can confidently explain the pattern that you follow in any influence situation. While the context may change, the model remains the same. This structure brings freedom and confidence to be present in the moment with others, free from anxiety, knowing that you're approaching the interaction in a way that builds trust and cooperation.

The structure comprises a series of communication frameworks or models that you'll need to commit to memory. These frameworks are proven to work and will give you a guide for your meetings and interactions, especially the difficult ones.

It's important to remember, though, that communication frameworks lose their value when they are used too rigidly. This book isn't meant to make you an influence ChatGPT robot. It's designed to help you authentically connect and inspire others.

Influence Earns You a Seat at the Table

In 2009, a client came to me with this challenge: the engineers in their company were viewed as transactional order takers for the business. In other words, people in sales, marketing, and the executive team approached engineering teams as subject matter experts who were useful for building solutions. But the company believed that engineers could deliver more value than just being order takers; they wanted engineers to be thought leaders and partners in the business.

Many engineers, especially experienced ones, reinforced the order-taker paradigm: they would talk in tech jargon rather than business language; they'd say no more often than yes, citing capacity or technology constraints; and they would offer quick fixes, because it felt good to get things crossed off the list.

The problem, as another client later revealed, was twofold. Despite the company's intimacy with the market and customers, requests and ideas for functional solutions were sometimes misguided and/or short-sighted. As a result, by some internal estimates, 40–60 percent of technology solutions weren't being actively used or managed; they were solutions still looking for the right problem. Furthermore, this dynamic tended to marginalize technologists during planning and decision-making: they were there to react to instead of forming the organization's goals. Many bright technologists therefore had no voice in planning conversations.

It's like the parable of the man who rescues a steady flow of drowning people floating down a river by throwing in flotation devices. Finally, he wonders why so many people are drowning; perhaps someone should run upriver to prevent them from falling in or educate them on the dangers of the river. But the man feels stuck, because he's good at throwing flotation devices. Besides, who would take his place to throw them in if he ran upriver?

Many functional leaders feel stuck in this paradigm. Functional experts across all parts of organizations feel stuck in their own silo of subject-matter expertise. Human resources shows up to do hiring, firing, benefits, and compensation. Marketing provides campaigns, branding, PR, and events. Finance is there to do reports, present financials, manage budgets. Salespeople get stuck with customers as "vendors." Support roles get stuck with colleagues as "admin."

_____ (*plug in your specialty area*) gets stuck with _____ (*plug in your primary stake-holder*) as a _____ (*plug in a transactional word that describes how you feel when you're just a functionary*).

To some degree or another, anyone in a sales, service, support, or delivery job is likely to be pushed toward the role of doer rather than influencer.

How do you get unstuck from reactively throwing life preservers? How do you get upriver?

Well, you could expand your technical expertise, gain relevant experience, work harder, or just complain to anyone who will listen. But those options will only reinforce the perception that others have of you as a skilled functionary who is victimized by email, meetings, and lack of resources.

If you don't have a seat at the table, let's face it: you're probably on the menu.

Develop Your Leadership Influence

I jumped at this client's request to help engineers because I had been one, and I had learned the secret to interacting with others as a leader and influencer. The secret was accessible to anyone with a growth mindset. It wasn't overly theoretical or abstract. It was practical, simple, and concrete.

I created a workbook full of well-researched, simple steps, case studies, and communication structures, provided examples of what they sound like in a real email or meeting, and left plenty of space for people to practice their own examples for real-world situations.

That first workbook has now been revised hundreds of times and has been used with thousands of people from Fortune 100 companies as well as small organizations across dozens of languages and cultures, including Asia, the Middle East, Europe, Africa, South America, and North America.

Recent participants have said:

- "I think and respond differently."
- "I build stronger trust."
- "We are much more focused as a team."
- "I've changed the way I build presentations and communicate changes."
- "We saved many hours."
- "I'm having much better conversations with stakeholders."

Whether you have official authority to foster change or not, the concepts in this book can help you build your influence and have greater impact on others.

Even if you're a student, a teacher, a politician, or a parent, you can apply these simple concepts to build greater trust and get others to be receptive and embrace your ideas.

We all have *yet* to realize our full potential when it comes to influence, but let me quickly acknowledge one thing.

Sometimes You May Need to Tell

Before we get into influence, let's agree on one thing: *sometimes you just have to tell.*

Influence works when the other person has the skill and will to engage in creative and collaborative solution-finding. If they lack the skill because they are new, underperforming, or in crisis, you might want to direct them straight to what's needed. Likewise, if they lack the will(ingness) because they are completely inflexible, have a bad attitude, or are unhelpful, again, you might want to tell it like it is.

What we're about to work on requires *some* level of receptivity and openness from all parties; it will also demand an investment from you. If you sense a very low level of skill or will in the area you're trying to lead and influence, consider closing this book, asserting your needs, and, if appropriate, discussing the consequences if they aren't met.

That's not what this book is about. This book is about helping someone engage with you to change their thinking in ways that build greater trust and impact. So let's get started!

Terms and Acronyms

Here is a list of some terms and acronyms used throughout this book for your reference.

CAPO. Criteria for considering whom to try to influence: chemistry, access, potential, outcomes.

CCCR framework. Cushion > clarify > confirm > respond.

Discovery question. Intended to elicit information.

Facilitated questions. Four parts: as is, should be, change, payout.

Four parts of human thinking. Desired outcomes; requirements and constraints; accelerators/hesitators; personal interests.

KPI. Key performance indicators.

PCE. Point, connect, evidence.

PTP. Positive > truth > positive. Formula for dealing with negative comments.

Reaction question. Engages the other person to reflect on what you've just said.

ROI. Return on investment.

PART ONE

Position: Setting the Table for Influence

CHAPTER ONE

Prioritize Availability over Productivity

Early in my career, I would walk to work through the streets of Boston. I took pride in how fast I walked. One day it was raining, so I was trying to walk particularly fast, that is, until a fancy Porsche sports car pulled up next to me, offering a ride. It was the CEO of the company I worked for!

"Hop in! I've got time to drive you home!" he shouted at me through the wind and rain.

I couldn't believe that this busy, powerful executive had the time and interest to help me get home.

In fact, he surprised me on many occasions with how he chose to invest his time.

For example, several times I remember being in a meeting that took an important turn toward product strategy or a customer issue and, lo and behold, our CEO would wander past the room, see us hotly debating, knock on the door, and ask if we'd mind if he jumped into the conversation. His contributions were always timely and welcome.

Of course, I became quite loyal to that CEO. In hindsight, I realize that a large part of his success was due to his invitational and available approach. Don't get me wrong: he was super intense and sometimes wouldn't be seen for days as he worked on a new partnership or venture, or perhaps just took time for himself.

But he rarely seemed rushed or anxious, which made others want to associate with him. As I recall, many of the people on his executive team had followed him from past companies out of loyalty and trust.

Now you might be thinking, "That's easy to do if you own a Porsche and run a company. I, on the other hand, have people breathing down my neck for deliverables and deadlines. I only *wish* I had time to wander the halls looking for a meeting to join. I'm in enough meetings already!"

Perhaps.

"It is easy for me to imagine," wrote Wendell Berry in his book *Life Is a Miracle*, "that the next great division of the world will be between people who wish to live as creatures and people who wish to live as machines."

Some days I pride myself on being a machine, walking as fast as I can, getting from one meeting and email to the next.

Several years ago, I returned home from work, and my wife asked me how my day was.

"Great!" I responded. "I got so much done—everything on my to-do list for the day."

To which she returned, "Is that how you measure your day?"

(Imagine me looking at her with a stunned yet admiring expression for such a penetrating question.)

Too often it is.

To the Harvard Business School class of 2020, the late Clay Christensen shared these words, which became the foundation for his best-selling book *How Will You Measure Your Life?*

When people who have a high need for achievement ... have an extra half hour of time or an extra ounce of energy, they'll unconsciously allocate it to activities that yield the most tangible accomplishments. ... You ship a product, finish a design, complete a presentation, close a sale, teach a class, publish a paper, get paid. ... [You] see the same stunning and sobering pattern: people allocating fewer and fewer resources to the things they would have once said mattered most.

This isn't just true about people who have a high need for achievement.

Most people, most of the time, will choose to do a thing that's *urgent* over a thing that's important.

Given the choice between having a difficult conversation with a teammate and responding to a few more emails, most people will do email.

If presented with an opportunity to take time away from work for self-improvement and networking, most people will opt to keep their heads down and continue working.

When tempted with the option of eating something available but unhealthy or preparing a nutritious meal, most will go with the quicker food.

People succumb to these urges for a few reasons:

1. Urges usually provide instant gratification—a sense of accomplishment or satisfaction.
2. People typically become accustomed to responding to urges rather than to more important things, so even if the urge is hard or unhealthy, it's easier to do, because it's habitual.
3. Urgent requests often come from people you don't want to disappoint. You say yes to the request or invitation because, as Cal Newport observes in *A World without Email*, humans

have developed a strong aversion to letting others down as a survival response. No one wants to let people down.

Responding to the Urgent Makes You a Doer

Look at your day today. Were you more of a doer or an influencer?

Not that those are always mutually exclusive (though often they are). When you are doing things that are urgent, you are often:

- Checking tasks off your list.
- Getting through email and other communication feeds.
- Pushing to get something done or delivered.

Creating, organizing, planning, delivering, producing, building, fixing, transacting, monitoring, reviewing, conducting, deploying, implementing, testing, responding, servicing—it's all mostly about getting things done. They're urgent.

Nothing wrong with getting things done, except that it usually distracts and derails you, reducing your availability to engage in important relationships and invest time in influence.

Availability: The Foundation of Influence

To have influence, you have to show up, speak up, have hard conversations, learn, and grow.

Influence happens when you prioritize availability over productivity. It happens when two or more people are communicating, presenting, discussing, listening and debating. It happens in quadrant 2 of the table below.

Over the years, time management and leadership experts have said that all human activity can be categorized into one of four quadrants on a 2 x 2 grid known as the "Tyranny of the Urgent" paradigm (after a book with that name by Charles Hummel) or the "Eisenhower Matrix" (after the late President Dwight D. Eisenhower, who used it as an aid for decision-making).

The Matrix of Urgency and Importance

1. Important and urgent	2. Important but less urgent
3. Urgent but less important	4. Less important and less urgent

In quadrant 1 (upper left: both important and urgent) are important tasks to be done immediately or soon. Those are important deadlines, assignments, crisis, and necessary obligations.

Quadrant 2 (upper right: important but less urgent) includes proactive investment in learning, growth, and relationships that usually requires scheduling and reserving time to complete.

Quadrant 3 (lower left: less important but urgent) gets in the way with its interruptions, requests, and temptations.

Here are examples of quadrant 3 when they come from other people:

Can you please take care of this?

Thoughts?

Did you hear about this?

Check this out!

And here are examples when they come from ourselves:

I suppose I'll just take care of this myself . . .

I'm going to let people down if I don't . . .

I'll feel better once I finish . . .

Oh, I see a new message came in; I wonder who it's from.

Then we slide into quadrant 4 (lower right: less urgent and less important), because we're stressed and need to escape to mindless activities, like scrolling our phone feed, looking at photos, the weather, sports scores, and so on.

Intuitively you probably realize that quadrant 4 is not the highest-value place to be, quadrant 3 robs your life of what matters most, and quadrant 2 is the hardest place to reach. You likely also realize that, when quadrant 2 is neglected, those activities eventually show up in quadrant 1. Here are some examples:

I was too busy to spend time with a top performer who was experiencing a series of setbacks, so he left the company for a new challenge, which means I now have to urgently hire his replacement.

I was too busy to proactively network and engage in the community, so my calls were colder when it came time to develop new business, which means I urgently have to do more prospecting.

I was too busy to stop and listen to my coworker talk about the challenges she's having with her kids, so I later had to work harder to urgently get her to help me with a project.

In nearly every case, it takes a lot more time, energy, and money once the activity moves from quadrant 2 to quadrant 1.

When it comes to influence, it's a bit like the Fram oil filter commercials from the 1970s, which said, "You can pay now [for the Fram oil filter], or you can pay a lot more later [for preventable repairs on your car]."

Likewise, you can pay now (by building influence, collaborating, making time for relationships) or you can pay a lot more later (by looking for new relationships and failing to gain attention or buy-in from existing relationships).

Imagine what might happen if you could spend less time in quadrant 3 and a bit more time in quadrant 2. Imagine that in the next week you are able to:

- Establish boundaries around your capacity despite the demands of others.
- Resist rescuing others or overfunctioning for them (doing things they can or should do for themselves).
- Tactfully push back or say no to unwise requests for your time and attention.
- Discern what's less important.
- Resist internal and external temptations.
- Discipline yourself to do proactive quadrant 2 tasks that are more important but harder.
- Move from being rushed and busy to being available and connected.

I'm not necessarily proposing a revolution in your calendar. Perhaps it's just an evolution. One extra hour per week in quadrant 2. What would that mean for your ability to lead with influence?

- Less stress?
- More relationships?
- Deeper connections?
- Better understanding?
- Less avoidance and attempting to escape hard things?
- Clearer thinking and communication?
- I know one thing for sure: this prioritization helps me live more like a creature than a machine. It allows me to connect in more meaningful ways with others—which directly leads to influence.

For example, have you tried to have a deep and meaningful conversation with someone who is busy? Doesn't work very well.

Have you ever opened up about your genuine thoughts and feelings to someone who is in a rush? Not so much.

Have you taken the risk to be really honest with someone who is multitasking, running late, or stressed? Probably not. Or if you have, it likely didn't go well.

If you want to have influence, you'll need to have meaningful conversations and get others to open up and be honest. None of that will be possible if you're living in the tyranny of the urgent.

Therefore, step 1 of influence is to loosen your grip on control and productivity and open your hands to the more proactive world of quadrant 2.

CHAPTER TWO

Build both Predictive and Vulnerability-Based Trust

I n his book *A Hidden Wholeness: The Journey toward an Undivided Life*, Parker Palmer observes that human beings—especially in group settings—often behave like animals in the wild, which remain in hiding and only allow themselves to be seen when it's safe and worthwhile to take the risk. The only difference is that with humans, the risks are social and emotional.

Harvard Business School professor Amy Edmondson explains that psychological safety is "a belief that one will not be punished or humiliated for speaking up with ideas, questions, concerns or mistakes, and that the team is safe for interpersonal risk-taking." In her research, she's found that leaders and organizations tend to outperform their peers when they foster this type of psychological safety.

Google, for instance, has found that its highest-performing teams are characterized by strong levels of unguarded, open, transparent dialogue.

That's not surprising. It's very difficult to lead with influence if you're hiding in the woods.

Satya Nadella found that to be true when he became CEO of Microsoft in 2014. Up to that time, the culture at Microsoft had fostered careful and cautious communication. Decisions tended to be made by those with positional or subject matter authority, and you didn't want to be wrong. Nadella realized that this style of communication was impeding growth and innovation, so he hired Carol Dweck to help him change the culture of Microsoft to one where people can freely admit mistakes, don't have to have the answer, and can relax in meetings, knowing others accept them as they are.

This mindset applied to all types of workplace communication, even when Nadella publicly apologized for insensitive comments he made when he was interviewed about diversity and inclusion in the workplace at the Grace Hopper Celebration of Women in Computing. A willingness to publicly admit his mistake and open himself to the criticism of others sent an early signal that he could be trusted.

Since then, Microsoft has made a successful transition to cloud computing and substantially increased its market value.

Aspire to the Highest Form of Trust

In his book *The Five Dysfunctions of a Team*, leadership expert Patrick Lencioni says there are two forms of trust in a relationship: predictive-based trust and vulnerability-based trust.

Predictive-based trust is when you trust someone because they are reliable and competent.

Vulnerability-based trust is when you trust someone because they allow you to let your guard down, to be honest, and to feel psychologically safe.

While predictive-based trust is very important, Lencioni explains that vulnerability-based trust is the highest form of trust in a relationship.

Social psychologist and researcher Brene Brown adds, "In my most recent research on courage and leadership, the ability to embrace vulnerability emerged as the prerequisite. . . . If we can't handle uncertainty, risk, and emotional exposure in a way that aligns with our values and furthers our organizational goals, we can't lead. Vulnerability is not weakness; it's our greatest measure of courage."

What might you see or hear in a meeting or interaction with high levels of vulnerability-based trust? Statements like:

- "Here's what I really think."
- "I haven't told anyone this yet, but . . ."
- "Confidentially, this is what we're thinking."
- "Let's hear what others have to say about this."
- "What are your thoughts?"
- "Our team can compromise on that for the good of the organization."
- "I volunteer to have that difficult conversation."
- "I feel anxious."
- "Here are some thoughts, but I'm interested in arriving at a decision together."
- "Let's be curious, not defensive."
- "I take responsibility for that mistake."
- "That didn't work, so let's talk about what we learned from it."

Saying things like this does require courage. It requires faith that others won't abuse your transparency, hope that others will reciprocate, and confidence that you'll be OK if not. This is the culture that Satya Nadella has been trying to build at Microsoft. It's a culture that makes it safe for people to be metaphorically *seen in the wild*.

What form of trust are you building with your stakeholders?

Vulnerability Leads to Influence

It's hard to get someone to change their thinking if they won't reveal all of their thinking.

When another person is guarded, careful, or withholding, it limits your ability to connect with them and speak to what matters most.

Furthermore, as we'll see in the next section, people commit most to change when they arrive at conclusions through discussion and contemplation. If they aren't willing to bring their thoughts and feelings into the open, it may limit their ability to process them. Sometimes people don't even realize they have certain thoughts and feelings until they say them out loud!

Most of us realize this, either intuitively or because we may have been hurt by someone that we were open with.

I'm reminded of the scene in the movie *Boiler Room* when Seth Davis, the young stockbroker, manipulates clients by preying on their fears and reminding them of their financial aspirations:

"I remember you saying something about wanting to buy a house, right? Well, how would you like to pay for it tomorrow, in cash?" he asks the nervous and excited client on the phone.

"Are you serious?" responds the unsuspecting client as he leans forward in his chair.

Yes, Seth Davis was serious . . . serious about getting the client to open up so that he could take advantage of him.

Whether it was by a salesperson, a girlfriend, a boss, or someone else, most people have been hurt by someone with whom they were vulnerable. If they haven't had a personal experience of their own, they know someone who has been hurt.

Ever since the Garden of Eden, people have been in hiding for fear of being seen and changed.

And that is the goal of leadership and influence: to see people for who they are and help them change to become what they can be.

You have to check your motives, though. Are you like Seth Davis, trying to make a bigger commission check, or are you like Dr. Sean Maguire, played by Robin Williams in *Good Will Hunting*, who pushes beyond Will Hunting's tough, protective shell so that he can help him have healthy relationships and realize his potential?

Dr. Maguire knew that getting Will Hunting to express his fears and emotions would get him to connect and cooperate with the good work Dr. Maguire could do in his life. In other words, vulnerability leads to cooperation and generosity.

In his book *The Culture Code: The Secrets of Highly Successful Groups*, Daniel Coyle describes what researchers call the "Give-Some Game": You and another person, whom you've never met, each get four tokens. Each token is worth a dollar if you keep it, but two dollars if you give it to the other person. The game consists of one decision: how many tokens do you give the other person?

It turns out that people will give, on average, 2.5 tokens to a stranger—somewhat inclined toward cooperation. However, in one experiment, subjects were asked to deliver a short presentation to a roomful of people who were instructed by experimenters to remain silent.

Coyle explains, "You might imagine that the subjects who endured this experience [presenting to a roomful of silent listeners] would respond by becoming less cooperative, but the opposite turned out to be true: the speakers' cooperation levels increased by 50 percent.

"That moment of vulnerability did not reduce their willingness to cooperate but boosted it. The inverse was also true: Increasing people's sense of power—tweaking a situation to make them feel more invulnerable—dramatically diminished their willingness to cooperate."

In my book *Four Patterns of Healthy People*, I talk about areas where I have personally grown, such as my anxiety with public speaking. I can relate to the feelings of vulnerability of those subjects in the Give-Some Game study, because I've experienced debilitating panic attacks in front of an audience. But from sharing my fears and my journey, I've become even more predisposed to cooperation and partnership with others seeking to improve their confidence and communication. Countless people have told me it has given them permission and inspiration to share their fears and growth. In fact, the first person who ever bought anything from me in my first sales role was the CEO of a successful company who let his guard down with me about his own fears once I signaled to him that I was trustworthy based on my vulnerability.

Here was this powerful, busy executive running a business, responding to someone half his age because I made it safe to come out of the woods and be seen.

That is the foundation of influence: foster an environment of sincere vulnerability, and everyone tends to be more cooperative.

CHAPTER THREE

Pay Attention to the Little Things

Animals in the wild tune their senses to any threats or environmental changes. Likewise, human beings process many signals from others, and the brain's amygdala activates what it deems to be appropriate fear or avoidance responses.

For instance, if I notice what appears to be someone multitasking in a meeting while I'm presenting, my amygdala will send a threat response to my nervous system, causing me to feel frustrated, annoyed, nervous, or insecure. Even though there may be other indicators that the person is paying attention, the human brain can only process a select subset of available data. As Harvard's Chris Argyris and others have pointed out, humans make assumptions based on select data and ultimately form beliefs based on the meaning and interpretation they give to that data.

How quickly do people select data and form beliefs about other people?

To support the launch of a new cologne collection, the Dollar Shave Club conducted a study on first impressions and found that seven in ten (69 percent) Americans form a first impression of someone before that person even speaks.

Could it be that people decide how trustworthy you and I are just by looking at us?

Princeton psychologists Janine Willis and Alexander Todorov would say yes. They conducted separate experiments where subjects were shown photographs of unfamiliar faces for one-tenth of a second, half a second, and a full second. A second group had no time limit for studying the photos. Participants were immediately asked to judge the person in the photo: "Is this person trustworthy?" or "Is this person competent?" They were then asked to rate their confidence level in their own assessment.

The researchers discovered that confidence ratings were highly correlated between both groups of subjects regardless of how long they studied the photos. In other words, judgments made in one-tenth of a second were basically the same as judgments made under no time pressure.

Out of all of the traits, trustworthiness surfaced as having the highest correlation between the one-tenth of a second look and an unbounded look at someone.

Fast impressions of trustworthiness go beyond how you look: they include your email, slide deck, and other collateral. In fact, three separate studies have shown that people make decisions about the credibility of an organization or product after looking at a website for only fifty milliseconds!

More studies and examples of the power of impressions can be found in Nicholas Boothman's book *How to Make People Like You in 90 Seconds*. One particularly interesting example relates to the importance of directing and opening up your torso toward others with whom you want to build trust. When your "heart" is physically obscured or blocked from someone, it may send subconscious signals that you're guarded, as you would have been in human history around an enemy who might have tried to attack you.

What Impression Do You Make?

These small examples (which are usually not intended to be overindexed as singular takeaways) form an overall impression to others that you and I are trustworthy.

What impression are you making? Here are thirty concrete examples of actions and behaviors that will help quickly signal your trustworthiness to others:

1. Smile or maintain a soft and welcoming expression, even when you're focused.
2. Mirror other's expressions, language, and posture.
3. Begin, as Dale Carnegie would say, in a friendly way.
4. Wear attire that shows you are thoughtful and intentional about your appearance.
5. Write emails and messages that are short and easy to read, understand, and reply to.
6. Avoid putting more than one person in the "to" line of an email, and limit the number of messages you send.
7. End professional correspondence with closed-ended questions (instead of something open-ended, like, "What are your thoughts on this?") to help people process your message quickly.
8. Show slides and other visuals that can be understood in six seconds or less.
9. Act graciously and supportively toward colleagues when presenting as a team.
10. Arrive on time or, even better, early.
11. Look people in the eyes and use appropriate greetings.

12. Turn your camera on for virtual meetings and make sure you're framed well in the screen.

13. Use a well-rated webcam, microphone, and selfie lights, so you're easy to see on video.

14. Use virtual backgrounds or ensure your background is not distracting.

15. Speak using relevant and easy-to-follow language.

16. Modulate your voice, and pause between words to allow others to absorb what you're saying.

17. Produce deliverables (documents, spreadsheets, reports, etc.) that appear professional and organized.

18. Demonstrate enthusiasm (a spirit within you) when you're communicating.

19. Communicate calmly, even when you're rushed or stressed.

20. Speak with confidence but not arrogance.

21. Listen more than you talk, and listen with empathy.

22. Ask follow-up questions that reflect genuine curiosity, never interrupting, one-upping, judging, blaming, or offering unwanted advice.

23. Avoid dismissive facial expressions like eye rolls, head shakes, frowns, and eyebrow furrows.

24. Try not to use letdown words like "unfortunately," as in, "Unfortunately, this is our policy."

25. Speak loudly and clearly enough that others can easily understand you.

26. Remain focused on the person talking.

27. Act more interested in others than in yourself.

28. Appear as though you care for your body.

29. Use inclusive language and address everyone equally.

30. Follow up when and how you said you would.

The list could go on.

Many of the items above can be and usually are demonstrated after an initial impression is made. They cover much of the ongoing impression we give others. They answer the nagging, never-ending question that the brain has been asking about others for all of human history: *is this person (still) trustworthy?*

Which of the items on this list would be important for you to further consider?

These are primarily "little" things that make a big difference and that typically have to be managed most when you're stressed, tired, or uncomfortable. I say "little" in that they are small, sometimes almost imperceptible actions, but they make a big difference. They operate like the degree of difference in water between 211 and 212 degrees, where boiling begins. They have the effect of one made putt in a four-day golf tournament that determines first over second place.

Taken out of context, that one degree of heat in water or that one shot on the golf course don't seem like a big deal. Taken as a whole, they often make a world of difference in how you're perceived by others.

Will your stakeholders:

- Open up?
- Speak up?
- Join up?
- Sign up?
- Listen up?

Or will they:

- Power up?
- Put their guard up?
- Check out?
- Shut down?
- Push off?

A huge part of setting the table (and earning a seat at the table) for influence is showing up to others as someone that they can truly trust.

CHAPTER FOUR

Be like a Salmon

Another key to earning and keeping a seat at the table of influence is to expand the frame of the lens when you're communicating.

Anyone that sells, makes, services, maintains, or delivers products or a service, or anyone who leads people or an organization that does those things, is constantly drawn to think and talk about the tasks and issues at hand. This is natural and usually expected by others who partner with you, work for you, or buy from you. The problem is that it positions you as a tactical advisor rather than a strategic partner. What's the difference?

A tactical advisor provides utility, and a strategic partner provides value.

Utility is useful. Your wireless phone carrier is useful. Your local fueling station is useful. Your dry cleaner is useful. These products or services meet short-term needs. They are typically chosen for their convenience, availability, and price. They don't generally lead or influence you to think differently.

By contrast, value is differentiated. Hopefully your doctor is differentiated. Hopefully your financial advisor or estate attorney is differentiated. Hopefully your faith leader, your kids' child care provider, and your closest friends are differentiated. These are chosen for their unique fit, their deeper appreciation of your needs, and their ability to push your thinking. Their expense doesn't factor as much into the decision to commit to them. The cost of switching is therefore high.

To be an effective influencer, sometimes you'll need to be a utility; other times you can differentiate. Sometimes a doctor just needs to run a test and send a prescription to the pharmacy, which is useful. But good doctors also take time to learn about each patient, build connection with that patient over time as they monitor biometrics, and offer words of challenge and encouragement to help the patient live their healthiest life. This is more about value.

The trouble with being a doctor, financial advisor, faith leader, child care provider, close friend, or someone in any other potentially high-value relationship is that those relationships can get caught up in the tasks at hand. *They can easily become reactive to urgent needs and requests.*

Doctors get busy, and patients come in not feeling well and just wanting a diagnosis. Doctors have seen enough patients with similar symptoms to smile, make a diagnosis, run the test, and be on their way.

Financial advisors also get busy, and clients call them wanting to place a trade or execute a transaction. Advisors have processed enough transactions exactly like this one, so they smile, get permission to execute it, punch the keys on their computer, and go on their way.

Doctors and financial advisors are incentivized to be productive. They make more money in the short term from urgent activities, they get really good at doing those activities, and, guess what, their clients ask them to do those activities. It only seems natural and logical that they'd do them.

The same is true for technologists who gather requirements to build an application. It's true for marketers who assess market needs to build a campaign. It's true for human resource professionals who run an employee survey and roll out a compensation or benefits package.

It's likely true for you. You're probably asked to build, sell, fundraise, service, deliver, or provide something to other people every day. You're paid to do that. The more you do it, the more efficiently you can get it done. The more you get it done, the more people ask you and expect you to do it.

The more you do it, the more you position yourself as a utility.

"No!" you protest. "I'm the best doctor/engineer/accountant/ banker around, and I care about people!"

It's possible you're overestimating the uniqueness of what you offer the world, but let's assume for a minute you're right: you're the highest-quality and most caring professional in your market.

Look back to the past ten conversations you've had with your stakeholders—clients, patients, partners. How much did you talk and ask about these things below?

- Their broader environment, the water they swim in. How much did you discuss trends in the space where they operate: their industry, their community, their family? If you're a project manager in commercial construction, how much did you talk about what's happening in your community's commercial real estate market, what financing and architectural trends you are noticing, and more importantly, what's happening in the specific industry of the organization you're building for?
- How they benchmark against their peers. How much did you explore their peers and competitors, along with how they are

perceived? If you're that construction project manager, you might talk about how the organization you're building for compares with others in their space. For example, if you're building healthcare facilities, you might discuss how this healthcare provider is viewed in the community and how they compare in brand, access, and outcomes to other providers in the area.

- Their game plan to maintain or improve how they stack up. How much did you ask about their overall strategy to gain competitive advantage, accelerate progress, or win? As a project manager, you might discuss the customer's or organization's approach in real estate.

- The progress toward their goals. Did you discuss the outcomes they're looking to achieve? Short-term and long-term measurables or milestones? What progress they're making (or not making) in pursuit of their overall strategy?

- The challenges they're facing in achieving those goals. Consider how much you discussed the obstacles in their way. Did you talk about constraints, such as time, money, capacity, and capability? In commercial construction, you may have talked about their challenges related to hybrid work or managing growth.

- Their needs to address their challenges. For construction, did you discuss space needs, parking needs, conference room needs, timing needs, financing needs? Did you discuss all of the requirements to make progress toward their goals?

- Wants that will make them happy. In the construction example, did you talk about aesthetics, location, and value-added options? Did you discuss factors that might slow or accelerate their progress toward the stated goals?

I understand that's a lot, but bear with me.

If you're like most people, most of the time, in most interactions, you primarily discussed the last two items in the list (needs and wants), with some reference point to the two before that (goals and challenges). Why?

First, that's what most people expect to talk with others about when they are contemplating any progress, change, decision, or investment. Whenever someone partners with someone else, they expect an exchange of needs and wants with a service, product, or deliverable. I tell you my problem, you tell me how to fix it, help me fix it, or give me the fix. I present you with my opportunity, you present me with advice, money, or capabilities so that I can pursue it.

To some extent, you and I spend most of our time talking about needs and wants because we get proficient at talking about them. If you're a project manager for a commercial construction company, you learn quickly how to talk construction and real estate development. You understand the factors that make a good deal or build. You get used to conversations about project scope, budget, and timing.

If you're a dog breeder, you get used to talking with potential owners about timing, gender, expense, and the health needs of a new puppy.

If you're a financial analyst, you get good at discussing budget allocations, variance, exceptions, and reporting.

If you're a photographer, you could practically have a conversation with someone in your sleep about schedule, deposit, venues and locations, pricing, and packages.

Fill in the blank:

I've gotten really good at talking with people about their _____ wants and needs, and how I'm able to help them.

One other reason why most people, most of the time, in most interactions will discuss wants and needs more than the bigger-picture areas listed at the top of the list above: everyone's busy. The fastest path to fixing, supporting, selling, delivering, advising, coaching, consulting, servicing, providing, and leading is to help someone fill in the gaps.

If they don't have time, you can do it. If they don't have expertise, you do it. If they don't have authority, you do it. If they don't have capacity, you do it. If they don't have the training or credentials, you do it. If they don't have answers, you provide them.

It's the barter that most leaders, coaches, educators, sellers, servicers and doers make with whomever they serve: show me your gap, and I'll help you fill it.

The better you get at filling gaps, the busier you get, because you're filling gaps for more people, advising others how to fill gaps, or paying attention to the things you bought with the money you earned filling people's gaps. Now you're busy, but fortunately you're fast at filling gaps.

Cut to the chase. Get to the point. Tell me what you need.

Ah, but what's the risk in this?

It's utility more than value.

You may really care about your clients, your stakeholders, or the people you lead, but if you're primarily filling gaps, you're offering short-term relief. You're a tactical advisor, and the costs of switching to another advisor are usually low. In other words, people are paying for your time or attention in advising them on tactics. If someone else can help them fill their gaps for less time or money, they'll likely shift away from you. Or if they've figured out how to fill the gaps on their own, they'll do just that. That's great if you've helped empower them, but it may mean losing the relationship. And if the gap goes away or loses its importance to them, they'll shift their attention to another priority.

There's not a lot of lasting commitment in a utility relationship.

If, on the other hand, you're able to talk regularly about most or all of the bigger areas listed previously, you position yourself as a strategic partner. You aren't just filling gaps, you're *partnering* with them in a broader and deeper context.

This is often just a shift in framing, like shifting your camera to get more in the picture, to include a broader range of view.

For example, I work with a team of technologists at a Fortune 100 company who are responsible for maintaining a large portfolio of technology tools that help their business operate and help their clients work with them. Wants and needs often surface from someone in the business for a new enhancement to one of the tools. This might be communicated to the technology team by someone like a product manager, who is responsible for designing the product and socializing it with the many teams that might need to use it. It might come as a one-off request, as part of quarterly "release planning" or in annual "roadmap planning." To position themselves as strategic partners in the business, these technologists have started to respond to enhancement requests with phrases like, "Sure, that enhancement sounds important. Let's discuss the broader context of this request so that we're able to optimize net promoter score and profitability."

At other times, these technologists are now proactively going to their counterparts in the business with suggestions for priorities and spending. They might, for instance, recommend investing time and money to address "technical debt," which are fixes and improvements that don't need to be made immediately but have a weight on the system performance or will "come due" one day when they limit scale or future performance. Or maybe they'll come with a recommendation to retire and/or modernize a legacy application. In these cases of tech debt or modernizing systems, they might start an email or meeting with language like, "Perhaps we could look at options for modernizing this system so that we are positioned to capitalize on the broader market opportunity available to our company right now."

Notice how these shifts in language change the frame of the camera to larger, broader organizational goals. They are the small steps required to move from being a mere tactical advisor toward being a strategic partner.

Again, this is not always easy. While it may not be hard to say something like "so that we can improve profitability and market share," it's hard to remember and have the courage to do it, because, as we've seen, most people most of the time in most interactions will talk about wants and needs. Therefore all the current demands press you to postpone the big-picture conversation for another time, when people seem more receptive or when we have more time.

Imagine salmon swimming upstream to lay eggs. Enormous water pressure drives against the salmon, but they know they need to get upstream for the survival of their species. They fight to not lose position, and they jump out of the water upstream.

If you're going to excel at influence, you need to be a salmon.

You need to fight against the inertia toward tactical gap filling communication. You need to fight against your comfort zone and your busyness. You need to fight against the expectations and assumptions of people you work with.

Let's go back to the image of someone standing on the shore of a river, watching people drown as they float past. At some point, an influencer will wonder why people keep coming down the river drowning. They might devise a way to get upstream to figure out why people are falling in but can't swim. They will broaden their context to address trends and circumstances, not just immediate needs.

You can be helpful by throwing flotation devices, but you have limited leadership and influence until you get upstream.

It's an investment in quadrant 2: the important but not urgent.

What If I'm Expected to Stay Downstream?

Many people reading this will say that this sounds great, but they are not allowed, invited, or able to get upstream for some reason.

Perhaps you're in customer support and you take calls from customers with very tactical needs, like solving a problem, booking a flight, or resetting their login. Calls are timed, and you're incentivized to get through as many as possible. How do you take time in those calls to get upstream?

Maybe you're an emergency room physician, an ambulance driver, or a firefighter, and you deal with urgent issues that require immediate hands-on attention. If you were to slow down the fire truck and ask the crew how fighting this fire addresses broader community issues, you would probably lose your job. If you were to stop working on a patient who has had a heart attack to ask them how helping them survive will support their overall approach to life, you might be at risk of a malpractice lawsuit.

You need to keep in mind a few things.

First, know when to broaden the context of communication and when to just be a very useful gap filler. If you're fighting a fire, it's not the time to contemplate the broader trends that have led to fires like these. You just need to put the fire out. When you're back at the station debriefing the mission, you can bring up the bigger questions.

Second, assess whether the people around you will be open to a broader conversation. Don't get me wrong: influence often requires challenging the ideas of others. We'll revisit that several times in this book. But sometimes people just aren't going to engage. If someone is in a rush or impatient or just doesn't appreciate you, they might not be ready for you to expand your value through a broader conversation. Hopefully this isn't everyone you work with all the time. If it is, you might want to consider your employment options. Hopefully you work with others who also strive for influence and, at least sometimes, will be receptive to bigger conversations.

Finally, there are times when, as Dale Carnegie said in principle 4 of his book *How to Stop Worrying and Start Living*, you need to "cooperate with the inevitable." Accept reality even if it doesn't conform to your desires. This frees you to release expectations that may cause unnecessary worry and frustration; it also opens you up to appreciate what is good and hopeful.

In a relationship, little things signal big trust. Knowing when you can elevate the dialogue and seizing those opportunities will show that you're not just a utility, you're a trusted partner.

Be a salmon.

CHAPTER FIVE

Use Value Language

When I lived in Ecuador in my early twenties, all my university courses were in Spanish. I lived with a family that spoke Spanish. Nearly everyone from police to taxi drivers to supermarket cashiers spoke Spanish. I wouldn't have enjoyed my time there nearly as much had I insisted on speaking my native language (English). Although it was exhausting, I tried to speak Spanish everywhere I went. Not only did I work hard to speak the language, but I tried to use local slang, mimic the local accent, and assimilate in other cultural ways.

Not everyone that visits or lives in Ecuador tries to fit in. Occasionally, I'd see tourists or business travelers dressed in clothing that made them easy to spot as gringos. I'd hear them in restaurants making no effort to speak Spanish or appreciate local food and culture. When this happened, I wondered why they wouldn't make more of an effort to connect. Arrogance? Ignorance? Discomfort? Apathy?

Whatever it was, they seemed to lose credibility—unless they were wealthy and/or powerful. Then they could use their currency to have authority influence. But they still didn't have leadership influence.

Leading with influence, as we've said, builds on a foundation of trust and connection. When you're dealing with people with a different language, culture, and preferences, you may need to adjust how you communicate.

Likewise, everyone has different language when discussing what's important to them. Some people value financial outcomes. Others value impact metrics showing how people or products make a difference. Others value functional outcomes related to their role or the type of work they do.

For instance, I work closely with a company in education technology. To them, the advances and methods in ed tech are very exciting. They believe strongly in the value of assessment tools, virtual learning solutions, and other educator resources. To work for them, you're required to demonstrate proficiency in their offerings. They think about trends in ed tech and contemplate their offerings and competitive advantages. They attend meetings about pricing, packaging, implementing, servicing, and hitting sales targets. You'd accuse them of negligent business practices if they didn't focus on these important factors.

Yet the educators and school administrators they serve don't spend much time thinking about these factors. Some not at all. They speak a different language and live in a different culture—the culture of operating schools and classrooms. If ed tech leaders want to build influence with educators and administrators, they need to talk and act like them. Their language needs to be centered around pedagogy, curriculum standards, test scores, teacher satisfaction, and graduation rates. As a result, this ed tech company hosts administrator conferences, they've hired many former educators, and they invest in training to help their teams speak the language that their customers value.

Differences in language, culture, and value can also occur *within* an organization across functional boundary lines.

Consider the case of the corporate communications and marketing department at a large multinational food corporation. Their teams spend their days with the media, advertising firms, and digital marketing agencies. Most team members come from a background in media, journalism, or communications. They have been trained to consider public relations, branding strategy, lead generation, and channel planning. Their work is measured in campaigns, promotions, and ad spend. But they work with sales, product, and finance leaders who do not share their language.

Therefore, when building influence with the sales team, the marketing team needs to think and talk about conversion rates, pipeline, account penetration, and market share. To connect with product leaders, they need to use language about product position by category, product placement strategy, quality, and net promoter score. When marketing works with finance, it's all about margin management, budget adherence, and cost of sale.

To be influencers, the corporate communications and marketing department trains team members to speak all these languages. They think of themselves as foreign diplomats whose success depends on their ability, as Dale Carnegie said, to "honestly see things from the other person's point-of-view" and "talk in terms of the other person's interests."

Consider what you provide to others and how they would explain what they actually value.

Interview Stakeholders Regularly

To improve my cultural and language assimilation into Ecuador, I took Spanish classes, read Latin American literature, and even took a class called Bailes Latinoamericanos (Latin American dance). I'm pretty sure the best thing I did, though, was to have as many conversations with Ecuadorians as possible. I'd ask questions, listen, and try to understand what they valued. Then I would affirm and validate the topics they raised or the areas they said mattered most to them.

Imagine you're about to embark on a study abroad experience with the people that you'd like to lead and influence. What movies would you watch to learn more about their culture? What are they reading that you could read? What classes could you take to look and sound more as if you belong in their culture? And, best of all, whom could you spend time with to more clearly understand what they value?

What stakeholder(s) do you have access to that could provide a line of sight to what they and those they work with value most? Consider trying to connect with someone in a position of authority and influence, because they often have the best perspective and clearest language about what matters most. Ask them out for a coffee or a short Zoom conversation. You might set it up by saying something like, "I'm reaching out to learn more from you about what you really value right now. I have a sense what that might be, but if I can more clearly align my efforts with you, I believe I can make a greater impact. Could we spend fifteen minutes discussing your current thinking around goals, strategy, and market trends?"

Perhaps that overture would be denied. Maybe you'd get a response like, "I don't have time for that. Stay in your lane, and keep producing your widgets for our team. We'll tell you how many we need and when we need them!"

Or possibly you'll get a response like, "You should already know this. Why are you asking me? Don't you watch our strategy presentations? Are you not listening to our corporate earnings calls?"

Or maybe you'd get no response at all.

While it's true that we shouldn't be asking about things we should already know, these responses are rude.

If this is what you get, consider soliciting support from another leader or finding a way to avoid working with this unhelpful stakeholder. At the end of the day, despite your best efforts, influence is never guaranteed. Some people just won't be receptive.

That said, it's worth trying. As they say, it's better to have loved and lost than to never have loved at all! Pursue even your intimidating stakeholders to show them you care and find out what they value.

In the stakeholder interview, you might ask questions like:

- How do you feel about the work our team has been doing?
- How does your team use what we provide?
- What results are you seeing from this work?
- What would you estimate is the return on investment of our work?
- What outcomes do you value most right now?
- How else can we build more trust with you and your team?

I've heard countless people describe the benefits of having this type of conversation on a regular basis, especially with high-level stakeholders. They not only gather useful feedback and set a pattern of open communication, but they clarify the words used to describe the goals of other departments, outside the company, or outside your natural environment.

Here are a couple of additional thoughts about speaking the language that others value.

Sometimes the boundary lines that invite you to translate your language are simply differences in personality style, demographics, or worldview. For example, a visionary personality may need to translate to details when speaking to a process person. Different age groups may need to consider what other generations value. And people of different faiths and politics need to translate what they believe into terms that resonate with others.

My friend Jeremy demonstrates this well.

He has started and runs multiple successful companies. Furthermore, most of the eight companies located in his office building are either owned or mentored by Jeremy. He sees great ideas and brings people and capital together to make them successful.

What superpower enables him to start, buy, or fund so many successful organizations?

It's his ability to communicate and connect with what people most value. Listen to him talk about the healthcare services company he started. You'll think he's been a healthcare provider for years, because he talks like one. Ask him about his wife's design firm, and you'll be amazed at how he understands the pressures their clients face. You'll also notice his company's focus on doing good for the world. Jeremy and his wife, Krista, who coleads the design firm, have invested enormous time and money in community development around the world. They speak a language that makes others want to work with and for them.

How does Jeremy know what language to use that resonates with what people value? He constantly asks and listens. Take him to lunch, and you'll be amazed, with all he has going on, how much he will listen and ask you questions about what you value.

Watch Your Jargon and Shop Talk

Another challenge that many people face when speaking the language of their stakeholders is using too many of their own buzzwords. To be sure, jargon and acronyms can be very useful shorthand when speaking with others who fully understand the terms, but too often leaders will use terminology that protects their power or hides their lack of understanding.

In his book *Leading through Language: Choosing Words That Influence and Inspire*, Bart Egnal writes that "jargon, buzzwords and corporate-speak usually exist because of a dearth of clear, powerful thinking" and that eliminating this language is "the only way that leaders can and do inspire others to act."

When you listen to highly effective leaders communicate, like Alan Mulally, the former CEO of Ford Motor Company and Boeing Commercial Airplanes, you tend to hear plainspoken language focused on what most people value. If you watch videos of Mulally, you'll notice that his language would be just as clear to a forklift operator as it would to a cardiologist.

Our team at work likes to call it "weekend language." Inspired by leaders like Mulally, if someone on our team presents materials that are too thick with jargon, buzzwords, or corporate-speak, we'll challenge them to use more weekend language.

When it comes to building influence, language matters. It is an important way for people to connect and transfer enthusiasm. If you're using language that's comfortable to you but less so to others, there's a good chance you're not influencing people that don't see the world the way you do or speak the language you speak.

Therefore, make the effort to translate. Consider yourself an expatriate working in a foreign land.

CHAPTER SIX

Talk like a Palace Builder

Someone walks onto a construction site and sees three people doing exactly the same activity. They walk up to the first person and ask, "What are you working on?"

"Laying bricks."

They walk up to the second person who's doing the same activity and ask, "What are you working on?"

"Putting up this wall."

They approach the third person and ask, "What are you working on?"

And that person says, "We're building a palace!"

Three people, all laying bricks, but they have three different ways of thinking and talking about their work.

Let's assume that all three have equal speed, tenure, and quality. Which of the three might have the most influence on the job site?

Of course the palace builder. Why?

Because the palace builder makes the connection between the work and the big picture. According to Gallup, knowing that your work aligns to organizational objectives and purpose is a key driver of employee engagement.

Also, the palace builder is less likely to get bogged down in details, can be more creative in problem-solving, and has a broader perspective on how everyone on the site fits into the project.

By now, you're probably saying, "Matt, we get it already. We've already agreed that it's important to think and talk about the big picture and end results!"

You're right: the palace builder is like the salmon spawning upstream. They are reminders to think and talk about strategic aims to build influence.

The palace builder is an especially instructive example, as it relates to how you set up communication, meetings, and discussions.

Let's see how to apply this principle in the real world.

Signals for Influence

Think about words and phrases that signal the type of conversation you intend to have. These may vary according to language and culture. For example:

- "You won't believe what I heard about Tony," signals you want to gossip.
- "Don't take this the wrong way, but . . ." signals you want to give feedback.
- "Let's come up with possible ideas to . . ." signals that you want to brainstorm.
- "Do you know how to . . .?" signals that you want advice or instruction.
- "You know, I've been thinking . . ." signals that you want to have a meaningful conversation.

How well do you signal that you want to have an influence conversation?

For instance, someone in one of my courses realized that most of her interactions with her company's sales team were transactional rather than being based on influence. In her role of reporting consumer insights for a consumer packaged goods company, she's regularly asked for charts and graphs to include in slide decks for salespeople pitching to major retailers. To shift the dynamic of these requests, she has begun signaling that she recommends more of a "palace conversation" as she responds to her sales counterparts.

On one occasion, when the account executive that managed the Walmart account emailed her a request for four specific reports to be included in a deck, instead of simply complying with or denying the request, she said:

> I'd love to work with you to ensure you have a compelling presentation so that we can drive more volume with Walmart and help them grow market share in this inflationary environment. Recently, I worked with another account executive on a different account and we took fifteen minutes to discuss the goals of the presentation and the context around the account. That resulted in even better decisions about what data to include in the presentation, which made their meeting more productive. Maybe we could do the same thing. Can we schedule fifteen or twenty minutes later this week to talk about what Walmart is trying to accomplish and how we can position ourselves as a partner for them?

As of a result of that fifteen-minute investment in palace-level discussion with the account executive, two of the originally requested slides were produced, with only one other slide that had not been requested but was conceived through the influence of the consumer insights leader.

Another course included several people who led content management and design for healthcare technology systems. Their counterparts in product and tech engineering viewed them as order takers rather than influencers. Their job was to write clinically compliant rules for how the systems would store, present, and process data. (Think about how Amazon has rules for storing product names and descriptions and presenting pricing and discounts.) The problem was that the content management team had little influence on product and technology decisions.

To increase their influence and involvement in important decisions, they came up with new ways of signaling their role and involvement when projects are set up. They rehearsed and drafted language like:

> We're excited to work with you on the buildout of this tool so that we can help decrease development expense and streamline future development in order to get new features released, which should lead to increased profitability. For example, we collaborated with product and engineering to move an antiquated database from hard-coded rules to a more flexible rules engine, which has led to much faster development and reduced expense. Maybe we could work out a more strategic approach to this system if we can consider new approaches. Could we schedule thirty minutes?

Another example came from customer success team members who would do regular reviews of their technology with their key customer points of contact. This meeting would invariably start with standard discussions about such matters as utilization, satisfaction, and requests for new features. In many meetings, the customer would make a request that would go something like this:

"Do you have anything that supports this need we're having?" or, "Do you guys offer services to help address XYZ issue?"

Not wanting to sound like pushy salespeople, these representatives would respond with something along the lines of, "No, unfortunately we don't," or "Oh, yes, we do. Would you like me to send you some information on that or have your account manager contact you about what we offer?" The customer would agree. If the representative remembered to follow up, usually time would pass, and the customer would have moved on to other pressing topics.

To avoid missing this opportunity, these representatives practiced a short signaling response to present their company more urgently as a resource for the need that surfaced. For instance, they'd say something like:

> Yes, we do help several other customers with issues like that so that they are able to save time and money. For example, earlier this week I worked with another company like yours who has implemented our XYZ product, and they are seeing great efficiencies in their operations. Maybe you'd find similar value. Can we set up a follow-up conversation with my colleague who works in that area to find out more about whether this would be beneficial for you?

The result from this change? Far more commitments to next steps with customers who are interested in expanding their relationship with the company, which is leading to an increased pipeline of opportunities and higher sales.

I'm also reminded of the general manager of a destination brewery who wanted to influence the owner to add food to the menu. Instead of focusing on the bricks (food, menus, etc.), he focused on the palace by setting up the conversation this way:

I wonder whether we can talk about a food service strategy so that we might grow revenue, strengthen our brand, and increase repeat visits. I've spoken with other brewery managers across the state that have been losing customers to new restaurants and distilleries. One, though, has added several food options through a partnership with a restaurant, and they have been able to not only mitigate customer loss but grow even while competitors come to the market. Maybe we could discuss approaches that might work for us. Can I schedule an hour with you next week to review ideas?

Notice something very important here.

The purpose of this setup is *not* to get a decision about offering food at the brewery. It's simply to invite a more strategic (palace) conversation with the others involved in the decision. It should cause them to enter the conversation in a more open, vulnerable posture rather than one that just wants to answer or argue. Will it set up a better conversation every time? Of course not. But it's much more effective than just saying, "You know, I've been thinking it would be great to offer food in our brewery. What do you say we look into that?"

That setup is fine, but there are two issues with it: (1) if the person isn't receptive to the idea, they will likely argue or reject it, which will shut down your influence immediately; or (2) if the person agrees with the idea, you may move too quickly to simply executing the idea, positioning yourself as a utility more than an influencer.

You'll have to decide on which setup is better. Sometimes it's OK to just be a utility. If you already have strong influence or if the circumstances don't allow for discussion, it might make sense to just say, "Hey, I think we should do this," or, "I'm going to go ahead and do this."

If you're right most of the time, your influence will likely grow, but less as collaborative influence and more as expertise influence. The latter is based on predictive-based trust more than vulnerability-based trust.

If you want relational capital, leadership influence, and vulnerability-based trust, you'll want to index conversations more heavily to the palace.

Elements of the Positioning Statement

Notice the pattern followed by each of the previous examples as they signaled a more strategic conversation. This pattern ensures you set up dialogue in a way that's:

- Strategic
- Concise
- Relevant
- Memorable
- Invitational

Do you have meetings, requests, or exchanges that tend to be transactional, oppositional, argumentative, or too narrow? Try following this four-part pattern. It is designed to be written in a short message or calendar invite or spoken in less than sixty seconds.

1. **Refer to the big-picture value or outcomes you're driving.** It's important that this first piece doesn't sound "salesy." You don't want to sound as if you're trying to close a deal by saying something like, "Would you be interested if I told you I might be able to save you $100 per month?" It's a leading question.

It would also sound salesy if you said, "I can help you improve quality while getting more done faster!"

That's likely to sound overconfident.

Instead, humbly mention value or outcomes that *might* be achieved by saying something like:

- "Let's consider approaches that might lead to increased revenue and market share."
- "I'm working with other teams on improving client satisfaction and retention."
- "It's possible there are some ways that could increase employee engagement and lower turnover."

One great two-word combination that can help ensure that your statement starts out focused on value and outcomes is *so that*. For instance, you might say:

- Perhaps we could discuss an idea for modernizing our ERP system *so that* we can drive greater efficiency and make better decisions across the org.
- Today we're here to look at a demonstration of these tools *so that* we might increase market penetration and pipeline conversion.
- Maybe we could schedule thirty minutes this week to talk about the pending org changes *so that* we can mitigate any regulatory risk and improve speed to market.

So that . . .

Those two words cue palace language. They nudge the conversation up the ladder of value. Make those your go-to words when setting up an influence conversation or meeting.

It will help you to be a salmon!

2. **Relate a quick success story or cautionary tale.** Consider the benefits of telling a very brief story—one that you can tell in twenty

seconds or write in two sentences. When you're setting up or inviting dialogue, a quick success story or cautionary tale can make others more receptive and can better position you as a thought leader.

Stories make what you're saying memorable. They also make it credible. Do you want people to believe what you're saying? Provide evidence in the form of an example. The more specific and detailed the story, the more realistic it will be. (Too much detail can make a story boring and hard to follow, so don't overdo it.)

Consider keeping a record of your good stories. I keep them in a notes app on my phone and try to practice them regularly so that I can remember them and tell them well.

3. **Suggest that it's possible that the outcome in this story can be leveraged or avoided.** It's important not to sound overconfident, because it might push people away, cause them to push back, or be overly skeptical. Instead of saying, "I *know* you'll benefit from this," or "You've *got* to consider this," just leave it open-ended. Use a word or phrase like:

- Perhaps
- Maybe
- It's possible

Say something like, "Maybe you could see similar value to this story."

This doesn't feel to the other person as if you're asserting your will on them. You're simply offering the possibility for their benefit.

4. **Invite a thoughtful discussion.** End your Positioning Statement with a request for conversation, not for an answer to a suggestion. You're not looking for a decision; you want agreement to consider and converse. As I've said before, use your judgment here.

If it's an easy ask and you're not likely to get resistance, maybe you do want to simply ask for agreement: "Would your team be willing to follow this process going forward?"

But if your request requires *influence*, if your suggestion will likely need people to change their way of thinking, you'll want to prompt thoughtful discussion. Ask a question like:

Would your team be open to joining our next meeting to discuss how we can collaborate for better results?

Can we spend a few minutes discussing the merits of a potential change to our billing process?

Could I schedule some time with you to talk about your goals and how this initiative might lead to better outcomes?

Those who excel at influence aren't pushy or bossy. They don't rush to a quick decision or answer. Their primary goal isn't to fix or rescue, it's to positively influence the way people think. If that's what you're trying to do—which leads to more sustainable buy-in—be *invitational*. Invite people to the table. Invite discussion. It doesn't need to lead to unnecessarily long dialogue. I've worked with pharmaceutical representatives who need to invite discussion with physicians between their patient appointments. The discussion might be one or two questions to get the physician thinking. But it's a conversation nonetheless. We'll talk more later about why that's important.

This is what all four parts might sound like if you were a shift supervisor trying to get your team to discuss a better process. The numbers are keyed to the points above:

1. Team, in our meeting today, let's talk about the changeover process when we need to build custom parts so that we can go faster, improve our quality, and ensure we keep this customer.

2. For example, two weeks ago most of you know we realized too late that we were missing parts in the setup for a rush order we received, which resulted in a lot of stress on our side and for the customer.

3. Maybe we could put our heads together to figure out a better way to prepare for situations like this.

4. Could we spend fifteen minutes in today's meeting talking about ideas and next steps?

In this example, you'll notice that the type of story was a cautionary tale. It was a warning to the listeners: we don't want to repeat something again. This can be helpful because it suggests that this could be a threat and should be avoided.

The one downside to a cautionary tale is that it can give people the sense that you're blaming or pointing fingers. Keep that in mind and, when in doubt, try to use a success story instead. Success stories can provide inspiration and demonstration of what's possible rather than what should be avoided.

Again, let's remember that the purpose of a Positioning Statement is just that: position. It sets up an influence conversation so that you can move to the next step in the discussion toward gaining buy-in and alignment.

Another Way to Set Up the Meeting

Positioning Statements can work well to generate a meeting, respond to a request, introduce an idea, or frame the discussion near the start of a meeting. In addition to, or perhaps instead of, a Positioning Statement, you might consider starting a meeting with a strategic agenda.

Many meetings, regrettably, have no known, clear, or followed agenda, making them a frustrating or confusing waste of time. Other meetings do have an agenda, but the items on it signal that the meeting will be more of a download than a dialogue or a tactical focus on the "bricks" that are being laid.

To avoid these pitfalls and position yourself for influence, after exchanging pleasantries, open meetings you're leading with a concise strategic agenda following a format like this:

1. **Mention the big-picture value or outcomes this meeting is driving.** In his book *Death by Meeting*, leadership expert Patrick Lencioni explains that most meetings are not engaging or productive because they don't clearly state what's at stake. Why is it, he asks, that we're able to stay engrossed in a movie for two and a half hours when we have trouble staying focused on a meeting for thirty minutes?

There are likely several explanations. One primary reason is that movies, like all good shows, theater, and books, establish what's at stake early. It's clear *why* you should pay attention. For example:

- An asteroid is careening toward the earth.
- The bad guys intend to make the heist.
- The relationship may not last.

Rarely are meeting attendees told clearly why they should care about the success and productivity of a given meeting in strongly meaningful terms. Especially recurring meetings.

How often do you find yourself in a meeting where people assume everyone knows the value of this meeting because, well, we have this meeting every week . . . or because you were invited . . . or because obviously we need to meet if we're going to make progress?

Far. Too. Often.

The result is conversation that gets very detailed very fast and confusing, marginalizing or annoying several of the meeting participants. Or the meeting gets into *fixing the problem* before everyone agrees on what the problem is or that time and money should be spent on it, leading to resistance, avoidance, and meetings after the meeting to talk about what people really think.

Do you want to extend your influence into the meetings that you lead or colead?

Begin by clarifying what's at stake with a statement like:

Ultimately the purpose of this meeting is to drive market share for our new product.

The end result of our time together should be greater efficiency for our teams as we work through the annual benefits renewal process.

The goal of this discussion is to help you advance your business objectives.

However you frame the big-picture value, it should signal that this meeting is helping to build the palace, not just lay the bricks.

The next step:

2. Enumerate the items on the agenda that you propose discussing. According to psychologist and neuroscientist Lisa Feldman Barrett, "your brain's most important job isn't thinking; it's running the systems of your body to keep you alive and well. According to recent findings in neuroscience, even when your brain does produce conscious thoughts and feelings, they are more in service to the needs of managing your body than you realize."

Therefore, your meeting attendees are probably thinking more about surviving your meeting or whatever else is weighing on their minds than about what you want to discuss. In other words, people in your meetings are preoccupied, distracted, and impatient.

To influence people in this state, you'll need to make the structure of the meeting clear, easy to cover, and interactive.

List the items on the agenda clearly and concisely, with sequential language like, "First, let's cover this, next, why don't we do this, and finally I'd suggest we do this."

Avoid phrases like "I'd like to talk to you about . . ." or "I'd love to get your ideas on . . ." Although the sentiment is fine, phrases like these signal that it's *your* agenda or *your* desire that's paramount. Instead, use words and phrases like "Let's" or "I'd suggest we . . ."

This language is also more inclusive and collaborative, prompting a mindset of working together rather than against.

It works well to signal in the first or second item listed on the agenda that you intend to "not so much seek to be understood as to understand," as the Prayer of St. Francis puts it. We'll get more into why this is important in part 2, although you can likely imagine the collaborative and inclusive spirit you will generate when you say that it's more important to you to listen than to talk, even though you're the meeting organizer.

For that first agenda item, say something like, "First, it would be great to hear from you on what's important to you and what you want to get out of our time," or "Let's start, if it's OK, with some questions about how this is going for you and what you think we should do."

Finally, consider grouping your agenda items into themes rather than offering a checklist of everything you propose to cover. This will likely make the dialogue more flexible and help elevate the conversation above a tactical list of to-dos. It will set the table for a discussion that brings people along to a new way of thinking rather than pushing your solution on them.

3. **Ask whether anyone wants to modify the agenda and it's OK for you to proceed.** This, of course, is another collaborative courtesy and a way of gaining permission to proceed with a more interactive approach.

I had a leader say to me once at this point in a meeting, "I'm not ready to talk! I just want to hear you present your ideas, and I'll decide whether anything is worth considering!" That wasn't what I'd hoped or expected, but I chose to meet the person where they were at, seek first to be understood, and earn the right to ask them questions.

Using this three-part pattern to set the agenda in meetings will further position you for influence.

Through your availability, leadership presence, psychological safety, and palace-builder language, the first step to influence is setting the table. Ensure that you've created a space that is inviting, welcoming, and generates dialogue, where people consider the bigger picture rather than just their own needs and biases.

Once the table is set, you can move to the heart of influence: probing, which we'll discuss in the next part.

The Reset

Clara's mind raced through the adjustments she wanted to make to how she was working and reaching out to people.

After just two coaching sessions, she was already realizing that she was trying to influence with expertise, hard work, and passion. While that was a natural inclination, it wasn't getting people to view her as a key part of their plans. She had assumed that because this initiative made so much sense and powerful leaders endorsed it, everyone would naturally give her the time and attention she needed.

Clara also realized that she wasn't necessarily investing her own time in the best ways by grinding out emails and documentation.

Then something beautiful happened. The parents of Clara's husband, Will, offered to take their kids for the weekend while he attended a rare weekend conference for work. That left Clara at home with only her own needs to meet (plus those of Larry, their basset hound, who didn't require much).

After a great workout in her basement and a shower, Clara poured herself a coffee and sat down at her kitchen table to write down key takeaways from her coaching.

Going forward, I need to:
- Delegate or eliminate weekly tasks to *free up more time* for this effort
- Proactively find time for *live conversations* with key stakeholders
- Place *higher value on communication and relationship building* versus mainly grinding out emails, presentations, and documents
- *Reposition my dynamic with John* to not be just a "utility" or "order-taker" for him
- Get key stakeholders to relate to me as a "confidant" more than an "outsider"
- Wear Agrifood swag, read press releases, and other materials from the industry, and show up for some company events so that I'm *seen as a partner*
- *Elevate my conversations* beyond simply my plan, needs, and requests
- Develop a *value-based Positioning Statement* for Agrifood and clients
- Write more *value-based emails* to stakeholders
- Start meetings by talking about the *value*

This initially looked like a long list of changes, but she realized it all blended together into two main themes: (1) invest more time in truly connecting with people and (2) position herself as offering value. She began with a proposal to John that used a Positioning Statement:

John,

I hope you're having a great weekend with your family. I happened to get a full day to myself today to get caught up, thanks to Will's parents taking our kids!

The coaching you got me into has really been helpful. Thanks so much.

In fact, it's caused me to think it would be great if you and I could connect on how we're moving forward with this effort so that we can accelerate positive environmental impact while also generating ROI for our stakeholders.

For example, last week I spent two straight hours sending detailed emails to Agrifood contacts and responding to your requests for documentation, though I don't feel we're any closer to getting support from Agrifood leaders to invite clients to our event.

Maybe we could talk about how you and I might collaborate together to ensure we're moving forward each week on our key priorities. Could we discuss this in our one-on-one this week?

Thanks,

Clara

In this meeting with John, Clara planned to discuss ways to offload some of her administrative work and adjust the agenda for their weekly one-on-one to be less task-oriented and more focused on progress around broader themes. She also wanted to see about getting an Agrifood email address and badge so that she could come and go at company locations, including the company store.

Finally, in preparation for the meeting, she wrote out the first part of her Positioning and Agenda Statement to Agrifood leaders:

> Support Agrifood growth by offering meaningful investment opportunities to clients so that *they* increase their ROI and *we* improve client retention.

Clara knew this would need to be tailored for each communication, but it gave her baseline language to include in emails and refer to in meetings.

For example, when she had her meeting with the director of IT to set up a landing page and database for her upcoming event, she started the meeting by saying:

> Thanks so much for collaborating with me to drive key organizational objectives that I know IT cares about, like client retention and continued top-line growth. Why don't we:
> - Discuss your perception of this offering and how it helps clients and Agrifood as a business
> - Talk about strategies for building the brand and communication of this offering
> - Determine next steps

Setting up conversations this way had the immediate effect of transparency, collaboration, and mutual gain. Clara found her stakeholders more eager to engage and more open to helping. She could feel herself evolving from an outsider with a great idea to an insider ready to partner.

She couldn't wait for the next coaching session.

PART TWO

Probe: Facilitating New Ways of Thinking

CHAPTER SEVEN

Explore the Four Parts of Human Thinking That Drive Influence

Once the table is set for an influence conversation, you have a choice: you can move to probing or proposing.

Proposing your idea, request, solution, or fix may seem faster. You've thought about it, and you may know the answer to the problem.

Yet neuroscience has proven that people are five times more likely to support an idea if they realize it themselves!

Also, someone might be coming to you with a request for assistance. While it might be efficient to simply propose how you can help, pausing to probe the need and context behind the request (after giving a Positioning Statement) will ensure that you're aligned to what's needed most.

Therefore, resist the temptation to propose. Instead, probe through questions. Questions are the path to helping people realize new ways of thinking. Influence questions should have greater value for the person *answering* them than for the person *asking* them.

In other words, it's important to restrain before you explain. Restrain yourself from answering, fixing, solving or telling. Instead, get them talking.

Great leaders emphasize prompting and probing more than proposing and problem-solving. There is an art to prompting and probing. In fact, many people see generative artificial intelligence (AI) prompters as one of the most crucial roles for leveraging AI. Ask better questions of ChatGPT or another person, and you'll get better answers. Better answers lead to better decisions and better results.

Philosopher Martin Buber explained that we have two ways of interacting with others: *I-It* and *I-Thou*. I-It is when you look *at* someone, and I-Thou is when you look *into* someone. I-It considers the other to be an object, a resource, a role, or a functionary, whereas I-Thou relates to the other as a subject in a relationship with depth and breadth.

This insight has enormous implications on your overall influence mindset. It indicates whether you're viewing another person (or group) as a transaction to be completed or a person to better understand. Even though you may have kind feelings toward those you influence, you may ask them about their weekend plans, and you may wish good upon them, it's simply a transaction if you're just trying to get them to do something for you or support your cause.

I find this to be especially difficult when I'm busy or rushed.

Just the other day, I had an idea that I needed someone to support, and I wanted him to run with it. I didn't have a lot of time, either. When I called him, he answered, we made small talk for a few minutes, and I launched into a quick Positioning Statement about the idea. I just wanted him to enthusiastically respond and say he'd take care of it, but he didn't. He offered counterpoints to the idea, rambled along in a stream of consciousness, and implied that I should do more work on the idea before involving him.

Ugh! I had a decision to make. Would I bail on the influence attempt in this call? Would I press the idea harder? Would I just make the ask of him, pleading, in hopes that he'd finally agree?

No, I didn't do any of those things. I took a deep breath and reminded myself that, with leadership influence, *slow is fast, and fast is slow.*

Rather than rushing the conversation along, I started asking questions to really understand his perspective, concerns, and desires.

I shifted my approach from I-It to I-Thou.

How Do You Know You're in I-Thou?

Brain science suggests that the two primary contributors to someone's perspective, concerns, and desires are, generally speaking, in the front of the brain and in the back of the brain. The front of the brain is known as the *prefrontal cortex*, which is the executive function or the more cognitive part of the brain. It processes information more logically and consciously and is considered more "modern," as it has developed in relatively recent human history. It also develops last in the stages of human growth.

The back of the brain, on the other hand, is generally the part of the brain which sits just above your spinal cord, with direct access to your nervous system. This part of your brain is deeply encoded with emotions, trauma, memories, and intuition. It sends impulses to your body to "eat that chocolate" or "don't touch that fire!"

As the neurologist Antonio Damasio explained in his book *Descartes' Error*, most people are taught from a young age that good decisions are made without emotion: the last thing you want is to have emotions intrude into the methodical process of decision-making. This view, Damasio writes, assumes that "formal logic will, by itself, get us to the best available solution for any problem. . . . To obtain the best results, emotions must be kept out."

Damasio's research destroyed that notion.

Building on the work of many neuroscientists in this area, Damasio studied people with damage to the part of their brain that processes emotions. He discovered that they often struggle with making even routine decisions. He found that *people lacking brain capacity for emotional processes could analyze a choice extremely well, but they could not commit to a decision.*

This finding implies that people with normal brain function make most decisions emotionally and rationalize them logically. Human beings use emotions to assign value and preferences to alternatives and ultimately shortcut the exhaustive use of logic to establish a preference.

How does that align with the PowerPoint presentations most people prepare to present their business case?

How well does it connect with the way most people justify their cause?

It doesn't. Seldom do people thoughtfully and purposefully seek to explore and discuss other people's emotions, even though emotions primarily drive decisions.

You'll frequently hear people respond to business cases and presentations from an emotional perspective. They say things like:

- "There's too much at stake."
- "Sorry, I'm not comfortable . . ."
- "This doesn't *feel* right."
- "It makes sense to me that we should do this." ("Makes sense" rarely implies a logical calculus.)

How do you know whether you're in I-Thou? It's when you are listening to the back of someone's brain. You're asking questions like:

- How do you feel about that?
- Why is that important to you personally?
- What's the win for you if we get this right?
- What's at stake here?
- What is causing you to hesitate in moving forward?
- What do you most value in this?

Listen Empathetically

I-Thou also empathizes with people's responses rather than just hearing them and moving on. This is where trained psychologists, therapists, coaches, and clergy usually excel. When someone says something, especially if it seems to contain emotional content, they say things like:

- Yeah, that's really hard.
- Hmm, thanks for sharing that.
- Uh huh, it's clear you feel strongly about this.
- Gosh, that really seems to be causing a lot of frustration.

Statements like these signal to the other person that you care, that they are heard, that you're with them, and that they are psychologically safe. You don't have to share their feelings or agree with the way they're feeling; you just have to honor and acknowledge.

Beyond that, empathetic listening asks follow-up questions that go deeper on provided responses. Simply asking generative questions like:

- Tell me more.
- Can you say more about that?

- Maybe you could expand on that.
- Go on.

These prompt people to go deeper and let their guard down, moving into I-Thou territory.

Additionally, empathetic listeners send other messages that encourage others to share emotionally, like:

- Nodding
- Making soft (rather than harsh) eye contact
- Maintaining a kind expression or subtle smile
- Keeping an open body posture, with hands visible and arms not crossed
- Repeating or mirroring back key words and phrases to affirm and echo what's spoken
- Occasionally summarizing what's been said
- Taking notes during or after an interaction, as appropriate
- Avoiding interruptions, advice, or minimizing what's being said
- Honoring confidentiality

Break Down the Front and Back of the Brain

Empathetic listening nurtures not only emotive responses but logical perspectives as well. Both emotion and logic contribute to people's preferences and choices. If you want to influence, you'll need to explore (and help them explore) both.

I worked with a team at a large health insurance company that was responsible for getting senior living facilities on contract with their health plan. While the company offered a compelling plan, many facility administrators were too busy to pay attention to another plan, or they seemed satisfied with the plans they currently had. To better engage these administrators, the team would focus time in every meeting to empathetically listen to both the logical and emotional considerations. They found that logical considerations fell into two categories, which we'll call *desired outcomes* and *requirements and constraints.*

The desired outcomes held by these administrators might be:

- Stabilizing their census
- Lowering hospitalizations
- Increasing length of stay
- Improving financial reimbursement

Whereas the requirements and constraints could be:

- Plan ratings
- Capacity for the number of plans with similar attributes
- Approval by the facility medical director
- Approval by primary care physicians
- Care standards

Both of these two lists are fundamentally logical. They can be measured, proven, demonstrated or achieved.

As this team empathetically listened to administrators, they would often hear more personal or nuanced aims that fell into two categories, which we'll call *accelerators/hesitators* and *personal interests.*

For senior living facility administrators, the accelerators/hesitators might be:

- Recent changes in facility ownership
- Negative previous experience
- No history with this plan's model of care and reimbursement
- Whether it's in alignment with broader corporate initiatives for a chain of facilities

Personal interests could be:

- Raising care standards for residents
- Job security
- Family member residing in the facility
- Personal financial gain

I know what you're thinking: "Delve into these personal factors in a professional meeting? Ridiculous! That crosses the line! I don't have time, and they would think I was wasting theirs!"

That's not what this group discovered with the senior living facility administrators. In fact, they found that often very few people, if any, were actually listening to the administrators' needs and concerns. Yet administrators are human beings just like you and me, working with both a head and heart.

Just a bit of extra thoughtful curiosity around these four areas netted an estimated additional $623,000 in the first year of empathetic listening. One team member estimated five new contract launches that year thanks to the application of this approach.

You might be tempted to think this works with administrators at senior living facilities but would never work with the people you deal with.

Well, how about dealing with scientists at pharmaceutical companies who are trying to commercialize and gain regulatory approval for drugs?

When a group of analysts that assists these scientists with research studies sought to engage more empathetically, they regularly uncovered these factors contributing to the scientists' thinking.

Desired outcomes:

- Getting their drug on formulary
- Evidence of drug efficacy

- Publication of findings
- Increased sales

Requirements and constraints:
- Urgent timeline
- Budget
- Data limitations
- Minimum sample size for generalizable conclusions

Accelerators/hesitators:
- Trust
- Likelihood of success
- Perceived level of analyst experience
- Getting questions answered that are "out of scope"

Personal interests:
- Job security
- Helping patients
- Adding to scientific literature
- Getting a bonus
- Proving oneself
- Appeasing the boss

What happened when these analysts explored all four of these areas? In their words:
- "I'm focusing more on the client's point of view and their business needs, not just the research needs."
- "A new client told me he chose our team to help him because we demonstrated being thoughtful."
- "This helped me save a project."
- "We identified the need for a study based on a new data asset."

This group of twenty-two analysts and researchers estimated $3.1 million in bottom-line impact to their organization by improving their influence in this way.

Perhaps you could have a greater impact on your organization by improving your influence. Maybe you'll be able to deepen trust and longevity with colleagues and customers through more empathetic listening. If you want this for yourself and your team, commit to probing for the four key parts of human thinking that contribute to attitudes about change and engagement. Two are logical, two are emotional. Two are in the front of the brain, two are at the back of the brain. Let me be clear that exploring the four parts of someone's thinking is not to manipulate them. Rather, it's to be on mission with them. Those four parts are:

Desired outcomes. What do they want to achieve?

Requirements and constraints. What is essential or getting in the way of change?

Accelerators/hesitators. What will make them feel better or worse about changing?

Personal interests. Why does it matter to them to achieve their desired outcome?

Helping others process and clarify these four areas provides focus and a case for change. In fact, as we'll discover in future chapters, you may need to refer back to these four areas as you explain your ideas for change and create urgency for action.

Few people will open up and talk about all four of these areas unless we've, first, set the table for influence and, second, taken the time to thoughtfully and empathetically listen.

Let's now look at keys to showing you're an empathetic listener who can explore these four areas.

CHAPTER EIGHT

Develop the
Art of Facilitation

I love Nordic skiing. Since I was a child, I've enjoyed classic style cross-country skiing, but early in our marriage, my wife and I took lessons to ski "skate" style. One tip from that lesson in Vermont remains clear in my mind. The instructor said, "The hardest part about Nordic skiing is maintaining momentum when you're going up steep hills. It's imperative that you keep your eyes focused on the top of the hill."

Why would this advice be so important?

When you're skiing uphill, the temptation is to look at the snow and your skis right in front of you. That's natural: it's where your energy is being directed and where your eyes naturally fix as they look straight ahead. But this can lead you to hunch forward rather than maintaining a strong posture. Consequently, you may lose alignment with the most efficient path forward as well as the motivating perspective of progress toward the goal.

When I heard that advice, I thought, "This is a metaphor for life!"

Too often leaders and organizations lose a strong posture, get off the path, or lose inspiration because they focus on the emails, the meetings, the checklists, and the problems.

Perhaps this is why a well-regarded executive coach explained to me that her system for coaching was simply helping leaders clarify their aims. She said that she provides little by way of advice. Executives typically have the answers already, and they know more about their business and situation than she does. She simply asks thought-provoking questions in this pattern:

First, she asks questions about *current reality*. What's happening now? What are the brutal facts? Where are you as you locate yourself on the journey?

Next, she asks about the executive's *aims*. The top of the ski hill. Where do you want to be? What's your vision in this area? What would be a great result?

Third, she asks about the *path forward*. What next steps do you need to take? What needs to change? What do you need to commit to, agree to?

Finally, she asks thought-provoking questions about *why change matters*. What's at stake? What difference will this make for you? Why is this important?

Her objective, she said, is to ask questions that cause the executive to think more clearly and deeply.

I've followed this pattern when facilitating dialogue too. I learned it in the Dale Carnegie "Winning with Relationship Selling" sales course.

For example, I used it with the leadership team of an engineering firm, who brought me in to discuss their issue of losing staff to competing firms. Instead of lecturing to them about the factors that drive employee engagement and retention, I surprised them by spending most of the meeting asking them questions.

1. How many people have you lost in the last quarter? What reasons have they given?
2. What type of firm do you need to be to make people want to stay? What's your vision?
3. How do you and your leaders need to change in order to realize your vision?
4. What happens if you don't change?

That last question in particular changed the tone in the room. The CEO responded from the head of the table. His voice got quiet, he looked down at the table, leaned forward, and said: "If we don't change, we'll keep losing people and ultimately lose to the competition. Our future depends on this."

He was speaking from the emotional part of his brain. Here was a logical, analytical, high-powered engineering executive speaking emotionally. At this point, I knew he (and likely the entire group) was committed to doing something about the problem.

Social science research indicates that when people arrive at a conclusion themselves, rather than being told what to do, they are more committed by a *factor of almost five to one*. Part of this is because people tend to be more invested in their own ideas and the work it took to arrive there.

The other reason is biological. Researchers at Medical University of Vienna's Center for Medical Physics and Biomedical Engineering and Goldsmiths, University of London, used fMRI scanning to understand the neurological impact of an aha! moment. Their participants solved a series of puzzles and pressed a button when they arrived at the correct answer for each.

From the brain scans, it was evident that the moment of insight in each participant was accompanied by a rush of dopamine into the nucleus accumbens, which is the center of the brain's reward system. As neuroscientist Christian Windischberger explains:

> Our results indicate a close correlation between dopamine, exhilaration, and creativity.... [They] provide the neural mechanisms explaining why the solution with an accompanying "Aha!" experience is more salient, facilitates long-term memory storage, and reinforcement.... An "Aha!" moment is, therefore, more than just a simple feeling of joy or relief but is a special form of fast retrieval, combination, and encoding process.

In other words, people literally *feel* attached to their own ideas and *stick to them* much longer.

The more you and I are able to help people explore the four parts of their thinking that contribute to their opinions and ideas, the more we're able to facilitate change and commitment. That's influence.

It's also why the executive coach I mentioned earlier is paid hundreds of thousands of dollars per year to meet with executives. Does she have all the answers? No! She's simply committed to the process of facilitating insights in the minds of the executives. Her questioning framework is designed to help people realize the gap between current reality and desired future. The aha! about this gap and the value of closing it fuels the person to change.

Imagine in your role as an analyst, manager, subject matter expert, controller, HR (human resources) leader, marketing executive, general manager, customer service representative, mother, board member, whatever your role(s) might be, imagine seeing yourself as an executive coach who seeks to generate aha! moments about the change that's possible (or necessary).

What would happen if your primary approach with your stakeholders was not to have the answers but to facilitate insights through better questions—to get them to fix their eyes on the top of the ski hill?

Now you could just be curious and work on asking more and better questions of any kind. That would be great! But if you don't use a structured pattern like the one from the executive coach, you may encounter a lack of efficiency and progress. I'll explain why.

Determining the Most Efficient Questions

It can be a fine line between asking too many questions and not enough. Many meetings have time constraints, and busy people don't want to waste their time. Moreover, people usually want to answer questions that are most *relevant* to having an aha! insight.

For example, I listened to a series of recorded customer service calls for an organization that provides payroll technology solutions. Sometimes you'd hear a customer service rep ask questions that were on topic but not germane to the discussion. For instance, a potential customer might say, "I heard about your company at a recent human resources conference in Las Vegas," and the rep would respond by asking, "Oh, do you do a lot of traveling for work?" or "How did you like the speaker at that conference?"

These are nice questions and could be considered rapport-building exchanges but typically don't add much value to the influence process.

Other times, questions were asked where the answer should already have been known. Questions like "How long have you been working here?" or "How many offices do you have?" can usually be found on LinkedIn or the company website.

Questions should incorporate research and past conversations. People want to be asked questions that move them closer to an insight. Perhaps it's the human desire for joy or progress through the realization of new ideas. Your flow of questions should give the responder a sense that they are getting somewhere.

I work with a human capital and talent leader who sought buy-in from her executive team to invest in leadership training. To get them to arrive at the conclusion themselves, she started by asking questions about leadership mistakes the executives had seen from their direct reports. Then she asked them to describe a vision of their teams operating at peak performance and whether they believed that their leaders had that potential. Next, she asked what they thought their leaders needed and how leadership training might support that. Then she closed the deal, so to speak, by asking them to describe the value they'd see if their leaders were to realize more of their potential.

The executive team sold themselves on the leadership training!

Do you see the flow? It's like the arc of a story. Here we are, there we need to go, this needs to change, and this is why it needs to change.

It doesn't have to go in that exact order. Sometimes it might make sense to start with a question about the vision (the top of the ski hill), then ask how that contrasts to current reality, discuss what changes need to be made, and dig into the benefits of achieving the vision.

Nor is it necessary to ask each type of question. Maybe you lead with one of the four types of questions and tap into the other three as needed. Sometimes people will just talk and talk after you kick things off.

Infuse Your Questions with Options, Insights, and Ideas

Matthew Dixon and his research team at the Corporate Executive Board (now part of Gartner) have found that influencers generally can be categorized into one of five types:

1. **Hard Worker.** Goes above and beyond. Self-motivated.
2. **Relationship Builder.** Strong customer service. Gets along with everyone.
3. **Lone Wolf.** Independent. Confident.
4. **Problem Solver.** Reliable. Fixes issues. Detail-oriented.
5. **Challenger.** Understands the stakeholder's context. Loves to debate. Pushes the stakeholder.

The most prevalent style, perhaps not surprisingly, is Relationship Builder, although only 7 percent of star performers fall into this category. On the other hand, Challengers account for the highest percentage of those who excel: between 40 and 54 percent. Regardless of your role, the characteristics of a Challenger can be relevant to anyone trying to influence.

One of the key skills and actions of the Challenger profile is the ability to *provide insights or ideas that push someone's thinking.* They frequently offer a contrary perspective.

Consider my friend Mike. He has excelled in his leadership roles at the Hershey Company because he's a challenger. You wouldn't know it when you meet him because he's one of the nicest people you'll find. While his humility and genuine kindness might lead you to guess that he is primarily a Relationship Builder, he's actually in constant pursuit of ideas that will help his business along with the companies that buy and distribute Hershey's products.

For example, Mike saw an opportunity at a major retailer that they sell through to improve their point-of-sale (POS) process. In his words:

> I put together a deck explaining the issue I'd identified along with an innovative approach to solving the issue and I headed out to Las Vegas for a retail technology conference to see if I could meet their CTO. When I found him, I asked him a few questions about his perception of the POS process and whether it was a priority to improve efficiency and reliability. He said, "Yes!" so I showed him my deck and asked him for his reactions, how he thought something like this might work, and whether he'd want to meet with another retailer who is working on the same thing. He smiled and invited me to join him for a meeting at their corporate headquarters, which opened many doors for our relationship with that retailer.

Mike doesn't have a background in technology. He doesn't sell technology solutions or POS consulting. He just relentlessly applies principle 17 from Dale Carnegie's seminal book on influence: *How to Win Friends and Influence People*: try honestly to see things from the other person's point of view. He also thinks through possible strategies and solutions that might help people. This makes him a Challenger.

Whether you're in sales, technology or finance, you can be a Challenger too.

The best Challengers are tactful and interested and lead with curiosity, not answers, though this curiosity is not devoid of a point of view. Challengers lead with a point of view, *not to give the answer*, but to catalyze clearer and more creative thinking.

You might want to challenge *me* right now: "Matt, you're telling me that I should seek first to understand before seeking to be understood, that the best leaders have good questions, not answers, and that people need to release dopamine in their brains by arriving at the conclusion themselves. Now you're telling me I should have a point of view and challenge?"

Maybe. Facilitation of discussion is an art. You'll need to decide for yourself whether your stakeholders need to be challenged to think more clearly and creatively. There's no doubt that by coming with your own insights, you run the risk of doing too much talking or missing the mark on your idea. That said, *if you offer your insights with humility in the context of discovery, you'll likely be appreciated for adding value.*

Four Types of Questions

Embedding your point of view in a thoughtful, questioning flow, like the one we've been discussing, includes the following four types of questions. The magic of this pattern comes in the tension that's established between reality and aspiration. When that tension is illuminated, the human brain naturally wants to see it resolved:

1. **As is.** This category of questions is about the current reality. Your questions can be about a specific product or service such as, "How is our team currently doing as your service provider?" but it's often ideal to elevate the dialogue. Remember you're a salmon. You're a palace builder. The best "as is" questions focus on the broader context. You might ask about feedback they're getting, how they and others are feeling, what's succeeding and what's slipping.

2. **Should be.** Here you shift to the top of the ski hill. Ask them to describe the "palace" they want to build. Prompt thinking about the target, the vision, or the ideal. As we've said, questions you ask should be thought-provoking, causing others to pause, look upward (a sign they're thinking), and say things like, "I hadn't thought about that" or, "Great question!" "Should-be" questions should also reveal a gap between what is and what isn't yet. As the author and consultant Robert Fritz suggests, people only change in response to a structural tension between a clear current reality and a desired future.

3. **Change.** These questions relate to the critical path from the "as is" to the "should be." What needs to happen? What does someone need to support, agree to, invest in, decide? It's in this category that you'd most commonly provide challenging insights or perspectives to catalyze new thinking. Your change questions ideally guide someone to establish the case for change and working with you to do it.

4. **Payout.** This type of question assigns worth to reaching the "should be." Because the answers to the change questions will surely cost money, time, and energy, the payout should provide the reason to incur that cost. Questions here could be positioned in the positive or negative (risk) side of the equation, such as, "What will be the win if we can make this change?" or, "What do we risk or lose if we don't make this change?"

When and How Do You Ask These Questions?

As we've said, it's best to (a) seek first to understand before seeking to be understood, and (b) allow the other person to arrive at the conclusion themselves. This means that many or most influence-oriented meetings will begin with some pleasantries, followed by a Positioning Statement and/or Agenda Statement, which will then move into questions (ideally for the majority of the conversation), followed by a few concise thoughts from you (as leader) about moving forward and next steps. (We'll cover those in the forthcoming chapters.)

Many conversations and meetings, however, will be more conducive to intervals of questions related to shifting topics or in response to what's being discussed.

For example, I work with the renewals and expansion team for a technology company. They schedule a regular series of reviews directly with the customer points of contact to discuss the progress of their implementations. Many customers will be implementing several products among the eight different ones offered, and time will be spent in these meetings discussing each of the products in use. They'll ask about such things as usage, feedback, and results.

There might be a set of as is–should be–change–payout questions for the overall customer situation, in addition to questions related to each product area. Customers will often inquire about other products or problems they are trying to solve. Although it would be tempting to respond to them with product information, the renewals and expansion team works hard to respond to a question with a question. For example, the customer may ask, "Do you have a virtual tutorial solution?" Instead of excitedly saying, "Why, yes, let me tell you about it and how great it is!" they will return a question like, "Why, yes. Can you tell me more about what's prompting your interest in virtual tutorials?"

Questions should be fluid, not mechanical. They should be the go-to communication strategy in any influence situation— more than talking, fixing, rescuing, or solving! They don't need to be long and complicated. Often the best influence questions are simple like "Why not?" "Can you elaborate on that?" "Why is that important?" "Tell me more." (I suppose that's not actually a question, but you get the point.)

These simple questions are examples of response generators: short, generative questions or statements to deepen, broaden, and elevate the responses you're getting. The goal, again, is to explore the four parts of human thinking that are driving choices and preferences while helping others get closer to realizing the positive change or decision they need to make or support.

People will not feel you're being an empathetic I-Thou listener if you ask too many closed or leading questions. (Closed questions call for one-word or limited answers such as "Is there an issue with this system?" "Do you like that feedback?" "Are you working to change that?")

Nonetheless, some closed-ended questions are just fine. Consider the 80/20 rule as your guideline: 80 percent of questions should be open-ended, 20 percent are closed-ended, still leading to meaningful dialogue.

How about leading questions? These assume an answer or are actually advice disguised as a question. Questions like, "Wouldn't you agree this is the right thing to do?" or "Have you considered switching to a new provider?" assume or expect an answer, which won't build vulnerability-based trust or psychological safety.

Oh, and try not to ask overused questions like "What keeps you up at night?" The 1980s called and asked why you haven't come up with a more insightful question than that one. (Sorry, the eighties were a great decade, but some things get old and overused, rendering them less valuable, like my compact disk collection).

Questions should facilitate vulnerability-based trust, so that the other person thinks or makes comments like, "I can't believe I'm telling you all this" or, "I've never really said all this out loud."

Comments like these indicate that someone is letting their guard down and plumbing the depths of their brain. This is a sure sign that you're entering I-Thou territory and building meaningful trust.

As we've said, your facilitation questions could be directed to either a person or a group. In a group setting, some additional considerations are often important for building the psychological safety for people to let their guard down and contribute to diverse discussion. This is especially true if one or more people in the group tend to dominate the discussion, hold a lot of power, or make others feel unimportant or disrespected. The Latin root of *facilitation* is *facilis*, or *easy*. Facilitation is the process of making something easy. Influence is about making it easy for everyone to think, communicate, and commit.

Here are some keys to making that happen in a group setting:

1. **Welcome attendees by name.** Especially in a virtual meeting, it's easy for people to appear without introduction or announcement. Whether they arrive early or late, take a moment to welcome them so they feel seen and somewhat accountable for participating.

2. **Avoid hybrid meetings.** When some attendees are present in person and others are virtual, it's hard for everyone to feel it's a level playing field. Often people have side conversations in person and can hear one another better than those attending virtually. If you do have a mainly in-person meeting with virtual attendees, make sure to continuously include the virtual people by name and ask for their contributions.

3. **In virtual meetings, encourage people to unmute regularly.** This is a best practice because people are so accustomed to being talked *at*, not *with*. People assume they can multitask or participate more passively if they are muted. Try asking people to remain off mute unless there's background noise

and/or unmute during all dialogue so they can be quick to contribute.

4. **Get people interacting in the first two minutes.** Challenge yourself to get people talking or contributing ideas to a virtual chat early in the meeting so that they realize that it will be more discussion than download. This can also be a great way to check where people are coming from. For instance, you could ask an opening question like, "What's your perception of what our team does?"

5. **Call on people without putting them on the spot.** Calling on people can be a very effective tool for keeping people engaged and gathering diverse perspectives. The key is to do it in a way that maintains psychological safety and doesn't waste time. Most people have seen this done poorly, where it goes like this:

John, what do you think?

John, you're on mute.

You must be double-muted.

OK, can you hear me?

Yes, we can, John. What do you think?

Sorry, can you please repeat the question? I was handling a customer issue.

This makes John look and probably feel ashamed and wastes valuable time. You can mostly avoid this issue if you start with the name of the person you want to call on and repeat the question two or three times with enough context for them to hear the question, think about it, and unmute. It might sound like this:

John, in a moment let's come around to you and hear your thoughts on whether we should proceed with the new CRM system.

While John's coming off mute, it would be great if others could formulate a response and consider writing it in the meeting chat.

OK, John, please unmute yourself and let us know your thoughts on whether we should proceed with the new CRM system.

It still takes a bit of time, but it leads to much higher psychological safety and higher quality responses.

6. **Don't judge or grade responses.** You're likely to disrupt trust whenever you say something like, "No that's not what I was looking for" or even, "That's a great question." In both examples, you're evaluating the answer rather than neutrally welcoming the contribution. The goal of a great facilitator is not to be smart and right. It is to make change and commitment feel easier to others, build trust, and help the person or group to advance toward a positive decision. Instead of grading the response, simply thank the person for their idea, summarize back what you heard them say, or build on their response by saying something like, "Yes, and . . ."

7. **Floodlight when you have too much spotlight.** Sometimes too much focus is placed on one person in a meeting because they are talking too long or are the focus of the discussion. This can create tension and discomfort, while reducing the time and space for others to contribute to the conversation. When you sense that someone is in the spotlight, you can floodlight to put the focus on the larger group by saying something like, "Thank you for that perspective, Vivek. What other thoughts does the group have about Vivek's ideas?"

8. **Smile and encourage.** Finally, people will feed off your enthusiasm and positivity. Even if you're not excited, energetic, or confident, consider putting some strength into your voice and some joy on your face. You might think that's unnecessary with the types you meet with, or you might think that is touchy-feely, but research shows moods are contagious. Mir-

ror neurons in people's brains will tend to reflect your attitude and engagement in the discussion. Low energy usually
leads to low participation, which usually leads to low quality.

Facilitation truly is an art to be continually developed so that
you can build trust and influence.

CHAPTER NINE

Summarize Regularly

Excellent listeners and influencers are skilled at summarizing and recapping. They might say, for example:

What I'm hearing you say is that you would like to win more deals and have greater impact this year. Is that right?

Regularly recapping what you've heard someone say shows that you're listening and ensures that you've understood accurately. It can also help people progress toward decisions, as they agree to what's been said up to that point.

Still more importantly, *if you can locate and distill the core desires of your stakeholders into as few words as possible, you have a key to unlocking future urgency and engagement.* Let's take a look at why:

Clarity leads to commitment. If people are confused, it's going to be hard for them to make a decision or commit. Too many details or factors will cause most people to defer choices or deviate from their line of thinking. They can get stuck in paralysis by analysis. On the other hand, if you can help someone boil down their thoughts to a core statement of desire, they'll be more likely to move toward it. This is why organizations spend time and money articulating a clear vision, mission, and values.

People lose sight of what they value. Great organizations don't just articulate their core aims, they codify them in writing, on walls, on their websites, and in meetings, because they know that people can easily forget what matters most. Former General Electric CEO Jack Welch said, "Talk about vision so often that at the end of the day you feel sick from talking about it." People get off track because of all the demands and derailments they experience throughout the day. If you can go back to a distillation of desire, you're golden.

The people you're influencing probably need to do some influencing of their own. Most of your stakeholders have stakeholders of their own. You may influence your child, but they may then need their friends to affirm their choice if it's going to stick. You might have gotten buy-in from your counterpart in engineering, but they may need to sell the idea to their team if it's going to happen. How do you equip them to socialize their new thinking? Give them lots of words and information? Of course not: they'd be unlikely to remember and even less likely to find a willing audience. You need to give them a simple summary.

Anything you suggest will be best received when it's linked to core desires. We'll get more into this idea later. For now, suffice it to say that anything you explain can now be said in the context of what matters. Consider again the words of Dale Carnegie: "Talk in terms of the other person's interests." What does this mean? When you speak, use language that resonates with the desires of others!

Times to Recap

I recommend recapping at four regular times throughout the course of ongoing interactions with others:

1. **At the start of a meeting.** Great leaders consistently refer to the big-picture value or outcomes toward which your conversation is driving. Whether it's a formal or informal meeting, whether it's a one-time or recurring meeting, you have the chance to frame the conversation in the context of the most important desires.

2. **During an interaction.** As you're listening, you can occasionally say things like, "So let me make sure I'm getting this right," "Here's what I hear you saying," or, "Can I recap what I think you've said so far?" This is especially useful to do before you transition into comments and suggestions of your own.

3. **At the completion of a meeting (or segment of a meeting).** Summarizing what's been said, and what's been agreed to, at the end of a meeting (or at the end of a portion of the meeting) can provide helpful closure and agreement before moving on.

4. **In meeting follow-up.** It shows diligence and strong follow-up when you can send a written summary to people after a conversation over email, text, or other appropriate channels. Most people appreciate having some documentation for reference. Just write a quick note that very briefly summarizes what they said was most important, like, "Sam, thank you for a productive meeting today about your goal to increase productivity in our newer markets so that we're able to satisfy the board pressure you're experiencing right now. Looking forward to our next meeting to review possible strategies!"

The goal is to regularly summarize what matters most to those you're trying to influence. This will lay the perfect foundation to move into explaining your position or ideas in a way that will maximize engagement and urgency.

What meetings or conversations are coming up where you could be more intentional about recapping the core desires of others in as few words as possible?

The Meeting

Clara realized that she was going into conversations seeking to be understood more than seeking to understand. It wasn't that she didn't care about other people's perspectives; she was just busy, excited, and driven to succeed. She heard a phrase that echoed in her mind: *go slow to go fast.*

The one-on-one meeting with John had gone incredibly well. Through the course of the discussion, which had taken on a more strategic tone, as if they were two peers discussing rather than transacting requests, John agreed to find a couple of Agrifood project managers to support Clara.

Furthermore, she'd gotten a different reaction from the director of IT than she'd gotten in the past from people in similar roles, who got tense when they were asked to provide support outside of their planned work. Instead, the director of IT seemed to think hard with Clara about how best to proceed to achieve optimal results. She confided in Clara to "be careful to avoid so-and-so on this effort" and "make so-and-so an ally in this, because he mobilizes change." The director of IT even revealed that she was maybe a year away from moving into the CIO role because of the CIO's pending (but unannounced) retirement.

Clara didn't have to *request* anything from the director of IT because she *wanted* to help!

"This is a mindset shift!" she thought.

In her coaching session, Clara wrote down that she needed to:

- Make *curiosity* and *questions* primary in her meeting agendas
- Listen for more *personal* and *emotional* factors that might be causing someone to move forward or hold back
- Be more *empathetic* in her listening by asking follow-up questions, repeating back to people parts of what they're saying and being totally present when others are talking
- Ask more and better questions that *create a tension to be resolved*
- Summarize key insights about the logical and emotional drivers motivating decisions

The true test of these aims would be her upcoming meeting with Leon Tripani, senior vice president of sales for the Agrifood bioengineering business. She asked about his availability for a meeting. After not hearing from Leon for weeks, she sent a concise follow-up note:

> Leon, please let me know if you'd be interested in a brief summary of an environmental and legislative trend that likely affects client retention and top-line sales for Agrifood bioengineering. This may factor in your strategic planning for next year. I'd highly value your perspective on how we should be thinking about this as a business.

Leon's assistant then replied to Clara, who got twenty minutes with him. Her goal was to convince him to make a strong push to invite bioengineering clients to her event, but she knew she needed to hold back on this request. "Build the case with questions," she repeated to herself.

The stakes were high, and time was short. She'd heard that if Leon supported this initiative, other leaders would follow suit. Twenty minutes to get it done.

Clara did her homework on Leon and the bioengineering business to ensure she could speak his language. She intentionally mirrored Leon's attire as much as possible. She'd made a point with Leon's assistant to book a room where they could comfortably sit adjacent rather than with elbows on the table facing each other. She also preferred not to be in his office, where the power dynamic favored him.

Clara arrived at Agrifood headquarters fifteen minutes early to get settled in the conference room. She remained standing until Leon arrived, being careful not to appear distracted by her phone. As soon as he walked in, she smiled, looked him in the eyes, shook his hand firmly, and thanked him for meeting. She also acknowledged that it was the end of a quarter and hoped they were able to finish strong.

"Leon," she began after they took seats on adjacent sides of the conference room table, "the goal of this meeting is to strengthen plans that result in higher sales and client retention by leveraging current environmental and legislative opportunities. To do that, I'd suggest in our twenty minutes that we:

"One. Discuss sales and retention factors.

"Two. Review any environmental and legislative trends impacting your business and clients.

"Three. Consider how these trends may impact the bioengineering business.

"Four. Determine the next step, if any.

"How does that sound?"

"It's fine, Clara. I'm happy to tell you about our business. Let me just say that we don't have capacity for anything new right now. Why don't you just give me your pitch and tell me what you need?"

Clara hadn't expected him to be quite so direct and unwilling. "I'd be happy to tell you more about what I'm working on," she replied. "To make the best use of your time, can I learn a bit more from you first? It would help me tailor my points to what you'd care most about. Plus, I'd highly value your perspective since you know so much more than I do about your business."

"OK, go ahead. What would you like to know?"

"Great," she replied. "I'm aware that consumer preferences continue to evolve and the market has higher demands for food biotechnology. How are you seeing this affect client retention?"

"It's a good question. Many of our customers, as you may know, are early-stage food startups who have a higher risk profile as they try to ride the wave (or create a wave) of consumer preference. This means we have to plan for a higher number of customers leaving, scaling, or adjusting ingredients."

"How would you ideally want to be positioning Agrifood as a partner to them through that early stage?"

"We want to be consultants, advisors, and thought leaders," he responded immediately.

"OK, that makes sense." Clara matched Leon's pacing, tone, and brevity as best she could while remaining nonanxious.

"Many of the founders of these companies," she calmly continued, "have come out of the university system and have strong sway with some of the key players in this space. If they could leverage their financial and political capital into some of these renewables projects, it could broaden their visibility and impact while seeing Agrifood as a key partner. How do you think that would be received by your customers?"

Leon paused.

"It's interesting," he replied. "I hear a lot from customers that they wish they had a broader public platform. They often believe that a stronger brand and a stronger voice in the community could help them shape consumer preferences."

"How could you see their involvement in the renewables space helping them broaden their platform?" she followed.

"Patagonia is a great example in the clothing space right now," Leon replied. "As CEO Yvon Chouinard invests and advocates for environmental projects, he raises the perception and visibility of their brand. He's forming consumer preferences and giving back to the community. Plus, if the legal and economic incentives are improving for renewable projects, it makes these efforts more compelling financially."

"To what extent does this idea support your personal goals?"

"I have a big personal push around client retention," said Leon.

"Fantastic. I think we can bring some value here as you position your team as consultants in order to drive higher client retention. Can I share some ideas on next steps?"

"I'd love to hear about it."

PART THREE

Propose: Making Your Ideas Known

CHAPTER TEN

Explain in a Way
That Will Resonate

Now that you've probed, you've earned the right to propose. Even if it was just pausing to ask a couple of questions, you've now setup the ability to propose your remedy or recommendation.

You may want to propose a point of view, a recommendation, an idea, a suggestion, an argument, or an update. You need to deliver it in a way that resonates.

Many times in real life, though, you find yourself talking too much, not being clear enough about what you want to say, or struggling to know how much detail your listeners want or need. You deliver your message the way it makes sense in your brain, but *your* brain is not *their* brain. And their brain does not have the patience to listen to you process information for very long.

Early in my career, I reported up to a very impatient listener. Occasionally he would ask me to meet with him, which was always a dreaded request, not because he was mean; he just had the shortest attention span I'd ever experienced.

With my background as a software engineer, I went into those meetings assuming the purpose was to give a thorough explanation or response to this leader's questions. I assumed he wanted me to be correct and make persuasive arguments. But he never listened to me for more than thirty seconds before it became obvious that he'd moved on mentally.

In hindsight, I'm glad I endured those dreaded meetings, because over time, I learned how to talk in thirty- to sixty-second chunks.

There are three reasons why people talk more than they should or more than other people want them to. It's almost always because they are:

1. **Emotionally charged.** When you're angry, excited, or nervous, your brain's limbic system has strong influence over your other thought processes. This means that the ventrolateral prefrontal cortex (VLPFC), which is your brain's braking system, is not very effective at getting you to stop talking. Therefore, you need to realize when you're driving in inclement emotional conditions, so to speak. Dangers like frustration, arguments, and hurt feelings may arise at any time. Be extra careful to hit the brakes if you start skidding off the road with your communication.

2. **Oblivious.** Other times, people talk too much because they don't realize that there's an imbalance in verbal contribution or that the other person doesn't care. This is, at best, lack of social and self-awareness, and at worst a form of narcissistic behavior.

3. **Controlling.** In many cases, people talk too much because it's a way for them to control the conversation, almost like a filibuster. The speaker will go on talking to keep the conversation focused on the topics of most interest to them. It can also

be a way of shutting down divergent views or attempting to control the thinking of others.

None of these are good reasons, because they don't build trust and often lead to a breakdown in communication. In fact, *you should very rarely talk for more than one minute at a time before allowing others to respond, acknowledge, and process.*

You can become a wall of sound, especially when you're anxious, excited or determined. It's not your listeners' responsibility to keep up with you. It's your responsibility to get clear in your own head and verbalize your thoughts in a way that's helpful to others.

Talk as if You're under the Gun

The best way to avoid overtalking is to imagine a shot clock or game clock ticking down every time you "get the ball," just like in sports. You probably have seen a shot clock, which is a large digital display of the time of possession each time a team gets the ball. If it counts down to zero, the whistle blows, and the ball is handed over to the other team. Quarterbacks and point guards know that they need to get the pass off in a short amount of time, or they'll get a penalty. Train yourself to do the same.

Consider the points that will have the most impact. In fact, start with the point that is most agreeable and understandable. "Get the other person saying 'yes, yes' immediately," said Dale Carnegie. The more disagreeable or complicated your initial points, the more likely the other person will reach a verdict sooner than you'd like.

Try to make just one point at a time. To continue the sports theme, imagine I'm standing a few feet from you with a basketball and I say, "Catch" before tossing it to you. Likely you'll catch it. But imagine if I threw three balls at you in rapid succession or at the same time. Some will probably be dropped.

Isn't it the same when people communicate too much information or information that's too complicated in too short a time?

If you just make one "pass" at a time, you'll more likely know whether it's been "caught" by your listeners.

This requires discipline and acceptance of risk.

Discipline means only letting one cat out of the bag at a time. Acceptance of risk means that you might have to chase the cat around the room and never get back to letting another one out of the bag.

What's the greater risk, though: the possibility you'll need to chase a cat, perhaps until the end of the meeting, by enduring others who might derail or hijack your line of reasoning, or that you'll keep letting cats out of the bag so quickly that no one has a chance to pay attention? In almost every case, the greater risk is the latter, because people are five times more likely to support your ideas if they arrive at the conclusion with or before you do.

One great way to make sure you give your listeners just one thing to think about at a time is to get in the habit of asking reaction questions every thirty to sixty seconds. Note I said *reaction* questions, not *discovery* questions. There's nothing wrong per se with a discovery question interspersed with your message, but in theory, we've already probed. Moreover, discovery questions are more likely to make you chase the cat around the room as you try to get back to your proposal. A reaction question simply engages the other person to reflect on what you've just said. In response, people might ask for more clarification, they may offer a counterpoint, or they might agree and expand on what you just said.

I remember getting into an unexpected debate on the phone with my colleague Kevin. After listening to his perspective on the topic, I quickly formulated my own three points to support my point of view. I began, "Kevin, one point here we need to consider is the fact that we already have something built that can meet this need. Secondly—wait, before I go on with a couple other points I'd like to make, what's your reaction to the first point I made?"

Surprisingly, Kevin agreed with my first point and took it in a different direction, which was much better than the other two points I was going to make. From there, we ultimately agreed on how to proceed.

Who knows what would have happened had I locked in on my second and third point before he had a chance to get the ball back? Probably we would have argued and wasted time; we might never have arrived at a mutually agreeable solution. At a minimum, he would have been annoyed at me for talking too much.

Here are examples of reaction questions that ensure we get the pass off before the shot clock expires:

How does that sound?

What do you think?

Reactions?

How do you feel about that?

This pattern of making quick points and turning them back for reaction is at the heart of influence. Even speaking to a large group and in more formal presentations, you can focus on one point at a time and pause for audience reaction.

It's the difference between a download and dialogue, between a dictum and discussion.

Making a point and getting a reaction ensures that you are:

In alignment. Checking in frequently is a bit like testing the temperature of food on the grill or looking at your GPS navigation while driving. It's a reference point that tells you whether you're on course, in this case with another person.

Handling resistance. I remember a banking executive taking me through his multislide presentation about the virtues of his bank. As each slide continued, I built up additional reasons why I'd not choose to bank with him. Rather than addressing my mental barriers, he pushed on, which pushed me further and further away as he spoke.

Gathering diverse perspectives. Have you ever been in a meeting where some people dominated and others contributed very little? Of course you have (even if you've only been to one meeting in your life). Some people process their thoughts verbally and others internally; furthermore, some feel psychologically safe to speak and others may not. How do you mitigate this problem and get more voices contributing? Check in regularly.

Ensuring you're understood and heard. Several years ago, I began an audio-only presentation of our company to a man who had agreed to take my call. Moments after I began presenting, I could hear him typing and making feigned sounds of interest like "Uh huh, yeah, OK, sure . . ." So I stopped talking after every thirty seconds or so and asked, "How does that sound?" He was startled when I asked the first time, obviously having nothing to say. After the first time, though, his typing stopped and he clearly paid attention. Whether it's due to the complexity of your ideas or the distraction of the listener, stop talking every thirty to sixty seconds to ensure people are with you.

Again, imagine that your meetings have a shot clock, like in basketball. It would be great if you could enable that function in virtual meeting software. Until it is, commit to mentally tracking yourself when you start talking.

PCE: Point, Connect, Evidence

Now what do you say in those thirty- to sixty-second windows? These can go in any order depending on what seems to flow naturally, but all three should be said before the shot clock expires and you check in. Let's take them in the order of PCE: *point, connect, evidence.*

1. **Make one *point*.** As mentioned before, state one point, fact, or claim that expresses your perspective on the message you're trying to deliver or the recommendation you're trying to make. For the reasons we've covered, you'll typically get the best results with just one point, starting with the one that's most agreeable and understandable.

   Points can be about any specific parts of your explanation that are helpful to advance the idea in the mind of your listeners. You might make points that explain your view or about how to implement the idea, when it should be done, who should be involved, what it will cost, how it will work, what it entails, and so on.

2. **Connect the point to their interests.** One of my favorite phrases for influencing someone is, "You'd mentioned . . ." It powerfully conveys that: (1) I listened to you, (2) I remembered what matters to you, (3) I'm helping you get what matters to you, and (4) this idea I'm recommending might just do that. To avoid sounding robotic, you can change "You'd mentioned" to similar phrases like "You've told me," "You expressed frustration about . . ." "It's come up several times that . . ." or something similar. Say this in conjunction with your point, and you become a true consultant.

3. **Illustrate and substantiate your point with *evidence*.** Want people to believe and remember the points you're making?

Hoping they'll take your words of wisdom to heart? Would you like them to be able to explain to others what they've agreed to do or change? Then add some evidence to each point. Tell a quick story, provide an endorsement from someone else, do a demonstration: something that will help them think, "Oh, yeah, I see that and believe it."

Which of these three—point, connect, evidence—is most important or least important to include?

Although your points are the most fundamental to your message, they typically come easily to the speaker and are more quickly forgotten by the listener.

In the late nineteenth century, the German psychologist Hermann Ebbinghaus published a theory based on a series of experiments at the University of Berlin explaining that human beings forget an exponential amount of information as time passes. To mitigate this forgetting, he posited, people need to have "spaced repetition based on active recall" and "better memory representation."

Connecting your points back to what the other person said earlier is a form of active recall and repetition of their own ideas and desires. Providing compelling evidence offers better memory representation. People don't need to remember your words; they remember your stories, illustrations, and research.

If you really want people to take to heart your recommendations, make sure to include a connect or evidence. People remember things most strongly when they clearly understand how it helps them and they can picture it in their minds.

This recommendation pattern will get a more positive response from others (or may not even be necessary) if we've asked great questions that have gotten people to realize the idea themselves!

What Does This Sound Like?

Putting the PCE—point, connect, evidence—together with the check-in every thirty to sixty seconds could sound like this, as it did for a financial advisor during an annual portfolio review with one of his top clients. I'll put it in context of an abbreviated version of the overall conversation. I've also noted in parentheses beforehand each concept that we've covered in previous chapters.

Hi, Brett and John, thanks so much for coming in for our annual review. (Strategic agenda.) As you know, the purpose of this meeting is to help you get closer to your financial goals in terms of sharing, saving, and spending so that you can live out your mission as a family in the world. To do that, let's:

First, hear from you what you two have been discussing related to money and what's happened in your life since we last connected.

Second, I can give you an update on what your money has been doing and how we're investing it.

Third, let's discuss some ideas and recommendations our team has for you.

Finally, we can determine next steps. How does that sound?

(Facilitated questions: as is, should be, change, payout.) OK, great, so what have you been talking about lately related to how you want to be sharing, saving or spending your money?

What's been going on in your life that has been driving those discussions?

What would you like to see happen in the next year with your family?

How do you want your children and grandchildren to talk about this?

What choices do you need to make in the coming weeks if you want to advance toward your goals?

How might you make sacrifices this year for longer-term gain?

What impact would that have for you two?

What's at stake here?

(Summary highlighting logical and emotional interests.) From what you're saying, you seem to know what you need to do this year in order to stay on track to saving for your kids' college while establishing a legacy of wise spending for your family.

(PCE 1 and check-in.) You know, I'd really recommend that you hold off on buying a new car this year. You'd mentioned this being a sacrifice you think you need to make. I work with another family similar to you in values, and they recently told me how glad they were that together we resisted immediate gratification purchases, instead planning out longer-term choices and legacy.

How does that sound?

(PCE 2 and check-in.) Another consideration is the money you currently have in your separate brokerage account. I'd suggest moving that money into the broader portfolio we're managing. You'd said that watching stock prices fluctuate in your brokerage account was stressful and time-consuming, and it hasn't been generating a lot of upside. If you compare the fee-adjusted returns of your portfolio with us and your brokerage account over the past three years, you'll see that your portfolio has a slightly higher annualized average.

What are your thoughts on that?

(PCE 3 and check-in.) One other idea to consider is paying down your line of credit, since it's fluctuating, and rates are increasing. You've told me in past meetings that you're debt-averse and want to be more free from financial obligations. You're paying almost $15,000 per year in interest on that debt, which in two or three years could itself pay for a new car.

What's your reaction to that?

These PCE combinations, followed by check-in questions, keep the conversation conversational and ensure that you're selling, not telling someone what to do.

In the meeting above, other pleasantries may be exchanged and other information may be shared and explained, but you can see that the influence portions of the meeting: (1) start with a focus on the palace to frame a broader discussion; (2) follow with facilitated questions to explore the four parts of human thought and get them thinking more clearly; and (3) land with ideas and recommendations designed to prompt positive change and choices. That's leading with influence.

Let's look at another example; only this time we'll see how the Positioning Statement sounds instead of the strategic agenda and how the PCE works when the elements are reordered. This example comes from a manufacturing company's safety department lead, who needs to get buy-in from the production supervisors to follow their safety protocols. Again, the specific techniques are indicated in advance in parentheses.

(Positioning Statement.) Team, as you know, we've been working on enhanced safety procedures so that we can reduce injuries and improve employee retention. For example, someone on third shift last week threw out his back lifting materials. He hadn't been using proper equipment, because he was in a rush. Maybe we can prevent more of these issues going forward. Could we talk about ideas we might all agree to lead and support?

(Facilitated questions: as is, should be, change, payout.) Sounds good. What theories do you all have as to why we've seen an increase in safety incidents?

How do factors like schedule, staffing, and timing of the production cycle affect safety adherence?

What does production look like when we're operating in an ideal way?

What's your vision for safety here?

What might be getting in the way of us more consistently following protocols?

What could you do differently to reinforce and lead this effort?

What difference does this really make to all of you?

What kind of impact do you think we could have on the business?

(Summary, highlighting logical and emotional interests.)

From what you're saying, I think we can reduce safety issues this year by all making a commitment to these procedures, which will ensure you each are recognized by your teams as leading a healthy and productive work environment. Here are a few things we could consider.

(PCE 1 and check-in.) For starters, you've talked about your concern that most issues happen when we're behind schedule. Because of that, we're printing these safety posters to point to on days when that's the case. We will be hanging these up in all areas in three languages. All you need to do is refer to them when you're behind schedule.

What are your thoughts on that?

(PCE 2 and check-in.) Since our biggest issue is sliced fingers, I'm suggesting that we now make these gloves required for everyone in production. You've all said that people complain about the gloves but privately express understanding of their usefulness. This just requires hourly spot checks to ensure compliance.

How do you feel about that?

(PCE 3 and check-in.) Evidence also suggests that we reduce incidents by approximately 10 percent per year for every 1 percent increase in reported communication levels on our employee engagement survey. That's a huge controllable opportunity. All we need to do is view our primary job as being lead communicators: listening to concerns, talking to team leads and others, and encouraging teams to talk about what they're seeing. You've said that part of your ideal vision for your shifts is that they are communicating more proactively and consistently.

What do you think?

The PCEs above are not in the standard order; in each, the point, connect, and evidence have been reordered to be more conversational and effective. Furthermore, there are three PCEs here for the sake of example, although there might actually be only two, or dozens of them, as the case may demand.

You can see in each a focus on the *others* and what *they* desire. Furthermore, they are concise, targeted comments designed to get the others reacting and moving closer to commitment. Each PCE should advance the thinking toward buy-in. If a PCE risks confusing someone's thinking or doesn't bring them closer to clarity, it's more than likely unnecessary.

CHAPTER ELEVEN

It's Not Just What You Say, but How You Say It

Since our kids were young, maybe six or seven years old, they've enjoyed watching presidential election debates. Although they had a low-level understanding of public policy at younger ages, they have appreciated watching how the candidates speak to each other and the audience. My children realize that these candidates are vying for millions of votes from different types of people and have been rigorously trained to offer a great presentation (which makes it entertaining when they don't).

My kids:

"He sounds like he's whining."

"Oh my, she's so defensive right now!"

"She looks like she's going to punch the other candidate."

"He comes across as so arrogant."

"I really like this candidate. She's so down-to-earth."

They are usually right on target with their assessments.

How could a "well-trained" communicator come across in a suboptimal way with so much on the line? Do they not realize that people won't vote for them if they don't sound confident, likable, and engaging?

Of course, sometimes policy and substance do win over form. And sometimes even bad form wins votes. But I'm sure you can remember candidates that never were elected to a top spot because they didn't speak clearly, or spoke condescendingly, or looked unlikable.

Research shows plainly that it's often not *what* we say as much as *how* we say it that gets us "elected." Quite often, appropriately channeled enthusiasm wins the day.

The etymology of *enthusiasm* is based on ancient Greek roots: *en*, meaning *in* or *inside*, and *theos*, meaning *god* or *spirit*. To have enthusiasm is to have a spirit within that's expressed outwardly. Everyone has different ways of doing this, and circumstances and topics call for different expressions. But in all cases, enthusiasm entails a spirit of interest in:

- The topic or solution
- The stakeholders
- Making progress or commitments

This might be genuinely communicated through:

- Facial expression
- Eye contact
- Hand gestures
- Posture
- Tone of voice
- Voice inflection
- Voice volume
- Pacing and pausing

Just like with presidential candidates, expressing productive enthusiasm in an appropriate way becomes most difficult when you're anxious. If you feel threatened, annoyed, stressed, or rushed, your vocal and visual cues might betray you. For this reason, it's essential that you:

1. **Decide before the conversation happens which visual and vocal cues will be important to demonstrate.** Making this decision in the moment is often too late. Go into the meeting saying to yourself, "Self, you know you frown when you're serious, so keep smiling when you're focused."

2. **Practice communicating in stressful situations with a coach.** It's not always easy to get feedback when you're in a stressful situation, but consider inviting a coach to watch a recording or listen live to a meeting, or ask for feedback beforehand from someone in the meeting whom you trust. Another option is to create simulated stressful circumstances. It can be challenging to manufacture the same anxiety that would occur in a real discussion, though it's worth trying.

3. **Manage your emotional condition before and during a high-stakes interaction.** What's in you often comes out of you when you're tired or under pressure. For instance, it will be quite challenging to demonstrate productive enthusiasm if you get behind schedule in the meeting or have strong pushback from stakeholders. That anxiety will find a way to leak out. Consider prayer, meditation, positive self-talk, journaling, exercise, or talking with a trusted colleague or friend to get your head and heart right before a big meeting or discussion.

Team Presentation Considerations

Often you are not the only one presenting ideas or recommendations. The influence patterns explored above can be a helpful guide for team presentations, providing signals to others on your team where you are in the process and keeping everyone aligned in the effort.

Specifically, PCE can be a great way to take turns speaking. In advance, you could plan who will talk about which points, and/or you could decide that each person with a speaking role will take one to three points before stepping back for someone else to take center stage.

Moreover, your audience—whether it numbers one or one thousand—will be watching how you complement and interact with one another. In a famous scene from the sitcom *The Office*, Dwight and Jim sit across from a reluctant buyer in his office.

While Jim is talking, Dwight makes a call on the buyer's speaker phone to their competitor's customer service line, and Jim follows by asking if customer service is important to the buyer. As the buyer says yes, you hear corporate "hold" music and an impersonal series of prompts from the phone.

Jim then proceeds to call their own company's (Dunder Mifflin's) customer service number on his own mobile phone, which answers immediately and cheerfully with a live voice: a very different customer service experience from the large corporate competitor.

This scene is great evidence for making the point to the buyer, but beyond that, Dwight and Jim are a perfectly choreographed pair (despite their history as office archrivals), and the buyer is clearly impressed.

Likewise, your stakeholders watch how you introduce, interact, and interplay with your teammates. They look for answers to questions like:

- *Are they coordinated and organized?*
- *What clues can I get about how they treat others?*

- *Is there mutual reinforcement of a shared position on this topic?*
- *Are they psychologically safe, or are they defensive or protective?*

Our nonverbal signals—not just to those we're trying to influence, but to the people that are influencing with us—can be key to a successful outcome.

A client asked me to watch a series of recorded Zoom calls they had done with customers to identify areas of improvement. Early in each meeting, my client's team introduced everyone on the call to the customer, and it went something like this:

Hi, Ms. So-and-so, it's great to meet with you again. I've got my manager, Jon, on the call today with me, along with Mary in customer service. Here's what I thought we could cover today.

This manner of introduction, I thought, made Jon and Mary seem like low-value tagalongs, so we practiced a more thoughtful approach:

Hi, Ms. So-and-so, it's great to meet with you again. I'm really excited that today I have with me two teammates: Jon has years of experience solving similar challenges to the ones you've discussed with me, and Mary cares deeply about seeing our customers succeed, so she'll be an invaluable resource!

The words matter here, but, even more, it's the way Ms. So-and-so sees how this team feels about, talks about, and thinks about each other. It sends the message that "we are trustworthy and here to bring value."

That's collaborative influence.

Meeting Facilitation

I recently participated in a meeting that engaged everyone and wasted no one's time. People joining from their home or office felt heard and seen. No one seemed to multitask. And the goals of the meeting were accomplished. Can you believe it?

In fact, I haven't just had this experience once. I'm starting to see it a lot, even with the meetings that are most tempting to decline. People are developing better strategies for virtual and in-person meetings. Are you?

It begins with the meeting leaders and/or presenters having the mindset that their number one goal in the meeting is to maximize engagement of all attendees. This is not *typically* the goal of meeting leaders and presenters. You'd think it might be, but too often it's to:

- Present all their material
- Make it through the full agenda
- Secure decisions, funding, approvals, etc.
- Disseminate information
- Strengthen their power, authority, and reputation

These objectives, on their own, rarely engage others. If you want to fully lead and influence, you need to take full advantage of virtual meeting technology and be an awesome facilitator. Here are additional ideas on how to do that, beyond what we covered in chapter 8:

1. **Keep your slides and points simple.** As marketing expert Donald Miller says, "If you confuse, you lose," so make sure people can understand your slides or comments immediately. Your slides should be digestible in about six seconds. To do this, use pictures, simple graphs, large fonts, and very little content. Don't include more than six bullets, and no more

than six words per bullet. If you're audio only, prioritize brevity. Only tell people what's essential. Let them ask you to elaborate.

2. **Continually go to the chat, polls, or whiteboard.** Most virtual meeting platforms include multiple layers of communication. People can send written messages, respond to polls, draw on the screen, use emojis, change their status, and split into separate audio groups. If you host virtual meetings with any regularity, you owe it to people to learn how to use these functionalities. They aren't gimmicks; they increase participation and engagement.

3. **Call on people.** As I've mentioned, I like to tell people upfront that I'm going to ask them to participate. It's important to do this in a way that minimizes discomfort. You can say, "John, in a moment, can you please come on audio and tell the group your opinion of this topic? You have a lot of background on this idea we've been discussing around employee benefits. John, what do you think?" Notice how I cued John to increase his attention and followed that with guidance for John's response. This should make John feel less insecure about being called out.

4. **Make people feel seen. Constantly.** Can you imagine going with a group of people to visit a friend's house and never being welcomed in or spoken to while you stand in your friend's living room and listen to them talk to someone else in your group? That would be awkward, weird, and deflating. Yet this happens all the time in meetings! People join meetings and are never welcomed or asked to contribute during the meeting.

    To the extent possible, make small talk until the meeting starts, continue to mention names throughout the meeting, and get people involved. Even if there are too many participants to do it with everyone, do it with some! "Ferah, Venkata, and Lauren, I would love to hear your perspectives on this. We don't have time for everyone to weigh in verbally, so please write your reactions in the chat."

5. **Use [destination] + "please" + [verb].** Virtual meetings have many cool ways to participate—chat, annotation, polls, etc. The key is to ensure people are crystal clear about what to do and how to do it. Give them a destination on the platform, like: "In the chat . . ." or "On the screen . . ." Then say "Please," so they view it as a request, not a demand, and follow that with a verb for what they should do: "Write an answer to this question . . ." or "Drop your pointer to the left of the bullet point that resonates most with you."

6. **Workshop real life.** In any meeting or presentation, participants benefit most if the content is directly relevant to their lives. Ask questions that people can answer about how the current topic or idea will relate to their work or life: "Where do you see this being useful?" "How does this relate to your current priorities?" "What are you working on that will be affected by this?" Then do some *workshopping:* ask people to come off mute and elaborate on their response. Talk through it briefly: "How do you feel about this?" "What will your team need to do to overcome these barriers?"

7. **Mine for conflict.** In *Death by Meeting*, Patrick Lencioni explains that meetings are dull and unproductive because they lack healthy conflict. If the word "conflict" makes you think "fighting" or "arguing," consider a different word, like "tension" or "differences." The point is to pull competing and opposing perspectives into the open. But people often hold back because the facilitator doesn't invite robust dialogue or for fear of consequences. Great virtual meetings foster psy-

chological safety, vulnerability, and diversity. Try asking, "Who else has a different perspective on this?"

8. **Keep reiterating what's at stake.** In his famous TED Talk "How Great Leaders Inspire Action," Simon Sinek says that great leaders inspire action by starting with "why." Clearly state the why of your virtual meeting and reiterate it throughout: "The purpose of our meeting is . . ." "The reason we're here today is . . ." This keeps people aligned and more open-minded to options. It also keeps you from getting mired in details that could be handled asynchronously or by a subset of attendees.

Aspire to make team presentations your chance to engage as many people as possible.

In summary, whenever you're explaining or recommending something, consider the percentage of time you're: 1) making points, 2) connecting to the unique situation of your listeners, 3) providing creative illustrations, and 4) soliciting reactions to what you're explaining. Balance all four of these and you'll increase the chances people will understand and support what you're saying.

The Pitch

Clara paused for a moment to look at her watch. She'd scheduled twenty minutes with Leon Tripani, and they were fourteen minutes into the meeting. Realizing it would be tough to get more time on his calendar in the next thirty days, she chose to be very clear and efficient with her explanation.

Clara had practiced parts of this conversation in the influence course she was taking. It had become apparent to her that when she was excited or anxious, she talked too long without pausing to allow for a response. She also realized that she needed to more explicitly tie her points back to the way they benefit her listeners. This, plus evidence and appropriate enthusiasm, would be the keys to unlocking Leon's support.

"Leon, let's invite your customers to this event we're hosting on community renewable energy investments. You'd mentioned wanting to position your team as thought leaders. We can send the invite to come from your team and they can attend side by side with your customers. How does that sound?"

"I'm open to that, but how's the event going to work? I've been to these before, and they've been more of a dog and pony show than actually having value for participants."

"At the event, we'll begin the main presentation with an overview of recent legislative changes. Then we'll facilitate a panel discussion of key renewable energy leaders. Finally, we'll summarize how attendees can invest and engage at the governance and policy level. This final piece, in particular, will give your customers an opportunity to broaden their platform, which you said might be important. Here's a draft of the presentation outline. What do you think?"

"OK, I think that would work."

"I can tell you more about the preparation, the event, and the follow-up, though we're just about out of time in our meeting. The next step here would be to work with your marketing leader to get the communication out. Knowing how busy your team is, we can do this for them. Think of us as consultants you've hired to help you with sales and marketing efforts. How do you feel about that?"

Apart from how Leon felt, Clara felt very confident. She'd stayed measured and conversational, which made her more relaxed and assured. Regardless of Leon's receptivity, she knew her ideas had value, and she was explaining them well.

"Clara, conceptually I like this idea. The challenge will be bandwidth, given our other customer-facing efforts. I'll talk to

Emma, who leads our marketing efforts to see if she thinks we can integrate this into our plans. Does that work for you?"

"Yes, of course. Thank you, Leon. When can we have another conversation about this?"

"I have my one-on-one with Emma early next week and will follow up with you after that."

Clara pulled out of the Agrifood parking lot while tapping her pump up mix playlist. She rolled the windows down and rested in the driver's seat.

"That went as well as it could have," she thought. "I can't wait to see Greta, Leif, and Erik, plus not have to make dinner."

Two weeks had passed since Clara's meeting with Leon. She'd sent emails to other Agrifood senior leaders but knew she wasn't going to get the attention she needed until she got Leon involved.

She texted John: "Still nothing from Leon."

Moments later John responded: "Call his mobile. You might get him."

Feeling hesitant and frustrated, she found Leon's number and called.

"Hello, Leon here."

"Uh, hi, Leon. This is Clara Daniels. How are you?"

"Oh, good, Clara. I'm sorry I haven't gotten back to you. My one-on-one with Emma got pushed out a week. I just spoke with her, and I'm sorry, but we have a few key marketing campaigns all lined up for next quarter. Plus, I didn't think of it at the time, but we are also pushing through a price increase around the timing of your event. Let's circle back in Q2 next year. Hopefully you can get involvement from other Agrifood businesses for this next one."

PART FOUR

Persuade: Managing Resistance and Tension

CHAPTER TWELVE

Be a Nonanxious Presence

Now that we've positioned an influence conversation, probed to understand the interests of others, and presented our point of view, it's time to persuade others to move forward with a change or commitment when they may hesitate or push back.

What type of pushback or hesitation have you gotten recently, do you get frequently, or do you expect to get soon?

Anxiety is perhaps the most natural response to tension and change. I witness it when I encourage my kids to practice their instruments, try to get someone to spend time on my project, or ask people to give money to a cause. They almost always react with some level of resistance and anxiety.

Leadership and influence are rarely easy.

How do *you* deal with the anxiety swirling about when others are resisting your leadership and influence?

We've all experienced it. If you're trying to offer any level of leadership and positive influence around you, people will get uncomfortable. With any idea that risks a loss of time, money, or reputation, with any proposed discomfort, pain, or extra energy, anxiety increases. Over time, anxiety leads to things like:

• Avoidance

• Isolation

• Partisanship

• Recurring conflict

• Blame

These symptoms of chronic anxiety are contagious, often spreading to the person attempting to lead and influence.

For example, let's say you're raising money for a charity. You reach out to a particular family because they have attended events hosted by your organization in the past, and you believe they are high-capacity donors. This family, however, is experiencing financial pressures at the moment and doesn't intend to give money to your organization. Nevertheless, they agree to attend your annual fundraising event because they have friends attending and feel bad about declining your invitation.

After the event, your follow-up calls and emails are unreturned. Privately they are complaining about your aggressive fundraising tactics. They finally write you an email requesting to be removed from your outreach.

Confused and put off by their "strange" communication pattern, you respond with an overly friendly and apologetic email. Internally, though, you're ruminating on what you might have done wrong and why this couple is so frustrating.

This example, which could be exchanged for thousands of similar stories unfolding every day with different details, is rich with anxiety on all sides:

- The family accepts the invitation without having the interest or capacity to give.
- They avoid follow-up attempts rather than just politely declining the first outreach.
- They blame the fundraiser for their discomfort.
- You passive-aggressively respond with an apology when you're actually upset.
- You repeatedly dwell on your confusion, hoping that by making sense of it you will alleviate your anxiety.

Why is all of this important for leading with influence?

Because the parties in this example all have substantially limited ability to lead and influence when they are operating out of anxiety. It's nearly impossible to build trust-based influence when you are fighting, flighting, or freezing.

This is why the great author, psychologist, and executive coach Edwin Friedman contends that the most important attribute for demonstrating influence is being a "nonanxious presence."

As the famous poem "If" by Rudyard Kipling begins:

> *If you can keep your head when all about you*
> *Are losing theirs and blaming it on you,*
> *If you can trust yourself when all men doubt you,*
> *But make allowance for their doubting too . . .*

This is the beginning of influence—to remain a nonanxious presence. Said another way, it's to be *nonreactive*. A nonanxious, nonreactive person does not adjust their values, preferences, or approach as a way of powering up, shutting down, or avoiding responsibility. A nonanxious, nonreactive person does and says the hard, helpful thing. They stay the course, they hold on to themselves, they remain solid and flexible.

Even if the other person fights your idea, pushes back, resists, avoids, or blames you, it's important to take a deep breath, remind yourself of who you are and how you got here, and proceed in a calm, thoughtful way.

CHAPTER THIRTEEN

Respond instead of Reacting

Being nonanxious gives you the capacity to listen and learn. If you are anxious, it's likely that you're either fighting (your guard is up to keep others out) or you're flighting (your back is turned as you try to escape). Being anxious makes it hard to hear and grow.

Cynt Marshall is a wonderful example of a nonanxious presence. In 2018, Dallas Mavericks owner Mark Cuban hired her to take over as the first black woman CEO in the National Basketball Association.

Marshall inherited a toxic culture. One of her first steps was to listen to everyone in the organization talk about their problems and frustrations. She met one-to-one with every employee. When it was tempting to defend, debate, or argue what people were experiencing, why it was happening, or what she planned to do about it, when she could have blamed the prior leadership, she just empathized instead. Marshall's leadership philosophy is: listen, learn, love.

As rock and roll star Bono writes about his own personal journey in his autobiography, *Surrender*, "If you want to change the world, you have to change the world inside of you."

This begins by managing your anxiety and remaining open to others rather than powering up or shutting down. Here are some strategies that might help:

1. **Reframe discussions from oppositional to collaborative.** Negotiation experts will tell you that good deals often fail because of ego. Two parties have much more in common than they realize, but they focus on where they differ. This happens because the paradigm of the interaction is oppositional: what do I have to give up to get what I want? Experts explain that you need to reframe the discussion.

Here's an example. Recently a client responded to my proposal by saying, "Your proposal is too expensive." (Note the oppositional frame.)

To which I replied: "It sounds like what we need to do together is find a way for both of us to feel comfortable with the investment."

Note the key words and phrases in my response and how that reframed the discussion from oppositional to collaborative. It's inclusive language.

This can also happen in physical spaces. For instance, the first time I met my dear friend and mentor Peter for lunch at a deli in downtown Minneapolis, I sat down with my food across from him at the table. He stood up, pulled his chair around to the side of the table, and said, "Matt, from now on when we meet, let's sit adjacent to one another, not across from each other. You see, the way you place yourself relative to others will create a subconscious frame for your interaction."

Nicholas Boothman and others have developed excellent resources that provide evidence and specific advice like this for body language and posture that sends collaborative rather than oppositional messages to others.

Using collaborative language helps all parties focus on ideas rather than personal agendas, which makes people less defensive and attached to their ideas.

2. **Remove shutdown and letdown words.** As we've seen, words matter. They can trigger fight, flight, or freeze responses in others, even though we may not have intended or realized it. Common shutdown words are *no, but, however,* and variations on this theme. You, of course, know why.

No typically ends the communication process. That's why, for example, improvisational comedy performers emphasize asset-based thinking. This means anything you "receive" in communication is to be viewed as worth something. You never reject anything; rather you build on it. If someone hands you a glass of water, rather than considering the amount of water that's missing, you focus on what's filled. This is demonstrated in the famous "yes, and" language pattern utilized in improv.

Saying "yes, and" in response to someone else doesn't mean that you necessarily agree with what they've just said. It means that you accept and receive what they've said, and you will build on their idea rather than contradict or negate it.

This way of thinking is essential in collaborative influence. It means resisting the temptation to say *no* or *but* and continuing with your counterpoint.

But could actually be an acronym for "before the ultimate truth": "It's nice that you just made a point, *but* now I'll supersede that with my point."

However, yet, and *although* can work the same way. These are shutdown words.

Similarly, it's important to avoid letdown words, as I've previously mentioned, like *unfortunately.*

Listen to customer service calls and you'll hear this all the time.

"Unfortunately, Mr. Norman, our policy prohibits that option."

"Unfortunately, our technology system doesn't allow me to do that."

"Unfortunately, it would set a precedent to others."

"Unfortunately, we don't have the available resources."

Do you see the maddening pattern? Do you feel the letdown? Do you sense the immediate loss of influence?

Replace unfortunately with something like:

- *What we can do is . . .*
- *A couple options we could consider together here are . . .*
- *That's an important issue you're raising. Let's talk about it.*

Words do matter.

3. **Use conversational language.** The Latin prefix *con-* means *with.* So conversational language is using words to talk *with* someone, not *at* them. Sometimes when people try to lead or influence, they use directive language. Directive language *tells*, conversational language *sells.*

My favorite conversational word is *let's*, as in "Let's consider another option."

Other examples of conversational language are:

- *Could we . . .*
- *Why don't we . . .*
- *Would you consider . . .*
- *Perhaps . . .*

These words and phrases keep people open and engaged, whereas directive language often has the effect of shutting others down or putting them on the defensive. Directive language is usually bossy, condescending or terse. Directive language might include:

- *You should* . . .
- *I need you to* . . .
- *Do this* . . .
- *Don't do that* . . .

Now you may be looking at this last list saying, "Wait, Matt, are you asking me to beat around the bush, soften my language, or become passive in how I communicate?" To which I would generally say, "No I'm not, that is, unless you are a highly abrasive or rude person to begin with."

It *is* often important to be direct. But there's a difference between being direct and being directive.

Being direct is clear and to the point. Being directive is bossy, condescending, and authoritative. Being direct is usually appreciated. Being directive is usually resisted.

So, yes, be clear and direct when appropriate, but make sure your language doesn't sound as if you're telling someone what to do, or they will not like it.

4. **Remain warm and friendly.** Years ago, when our boys were young, our neighbor approached me and said, "Matt, I just had scratches and dents repaired on my car that were caused by your sons riding their bikes in my driveway. It cost me $200, and I'd like you to reimburse me."

He handed me the invoice from the auto body repair location to solidify his point.

Although we had a good relationship with our neighbor, this request set me off. I immediately felt defensive, with thoughts like:

"Are you sure it was our kids, with so many other kids their age riding bikes in the neighborhood?"

"Do you have any proof or surveillance footage?"

"Why would you get the repairs done without consulting with me first?"

Fortunately, none of those questions came out of my mouth, as they all would have sounded defensive and would have been unproductive.

Instead, I said, "Rob, the most important thing here is our relationship as neighbors."

This technique was impressed upon me by my dad, who generally is very good at diffusing tension and building trust. When faced with conflict, he'd challenge me to consider *what matters most.*

With my neighbor, the quality of our relationship mattered much more than the $200. This reminder gave me the capacity to respond the way I did, which kept both of us open to an amicable solution. Instead of arguing, I said, "Rob, since we haven't actually seen my boys cause this damage and since my boys say they didn't do it, how about I pay half? I'll give you the neighborhood directory and invite you to contact other families with young kids to see if they'd contribute toward the other half."

That satisfied both of us.

Dale Carnegie said, "I have come to the conclusion that there is only one way under high heaven to get the best of an argument—and that is to avoid it."

Remind yourself what matters most. It's rarely winning an argument.

5. **Appeal to noble motives.** Good politicians do this all the time. In the face of partisan division, they will exclaim: "We need to do this for the environment . . . for our children . . . for our country!"

If you're faced with partisan politics in your organization, or even just with someone who has different opinions, emphasize the greater shared motivation. Philosophers and strategists have often referred to these shared agreements as *first principles*.

Financier J. P. Morgan once observed that a person always has two reasons for doing anything: a good reason and the real reason. Highlight the good reason—the reason that's common to most of the people involved. As Dale Carnegie wrote, we should "appeal to the nobler motives."

What might that be for you? It could be:
- What's best for the customer
- What unites our teams
- The spirit of innovation
- Alignment with our values
- Part of our strategic plan
- A gift to our future selves

Highlighting noble motives will also tend to make people less anxious about losing or giving up something.

In 1995, Andy Grove, the CEO of the technology company Intel, convinced Steve Jobs, then CEO of Pixar Animation Studios, to do a partnership by saying, "Hey, not only have I helped you in the past, but you're missing a chance *to do something bigger than money here—to help push the industry forward.*"

This ended up persuading Jobs to change his point of view.

As Bono wrote in his biography, "The search for common ground starts with the search for higher ground. Even with your opponents. Especially with your opponents. You don't have to agree on everything if the one thing you do agree on is important enough."

6. **Respond instead of reacting.** The difference between responding and reacting, you might say, is communicating thoughtfully
versus emotionally. While it can often be helpful to express your
emotions, being emotional usually means having less control over
your words. They come out in the way a young child might communicate who hasn't developed the capacity to filter and manage
their thoughts.

Generally, pharmacists would say you want to *respond* to a
medication, not *react* to it; having a *reaction* to a food or medication results in unhealthy outcomes. Likewise, a *chain reaction* is
usually something uncontrolled and often unwanted.

This can be a helpful way of evaluating your thoughts, words,
and actions: ask yourself, "Self, am I responding or reacting right
now?"

If you're abruptly changing your values, preferences, or methods to have your short-term emotional needs met, you're likely
reacting. Conversely, if you're thinking about your values and the
greater good and are trying to be curious about all angles, you're
probably responding.

As we've already seen, being nonreactive may be the most
essential part of strong leadership and influence.

7. **Manage your physiology.** Underlying the ability to implement
the ideas above is the need to stay physically and mentally fit for
service. If your breathing is rapid and shallow, if your muscles are
tense, if your face is frowning and you generally feel unnerved, it's
going to be hard to maintain a thoughtful approach.

One way to do this is by understanding and managing your
breath, as James Nestor observes in his book *Breath: The New Science of a Lost Art.* Simply paying attention to your breath, breathing
in for a count of four and out for a count of four, inhaling through

your nose, can be a great start. This is proved to lower your heart rate and mitigate the fight, flight, or freeze response.

8. **Relocate, restore, or ask for a redo.** *Relocating* refers to the fact that sometimes the physical or virtual space we are in can add to the stress and tension. If the space has a power dynamic, a bias toward one party, a history, or just isn't conducive to relaxed dialogue, you may want to move venue, if that's possible.

You also may need to restore yourself to physical and emotional equilibrium by taking some extra time to process what you're thinking and feeling. If you're feeling off balance or are not responding in the most productive way, consider telling others involved that you'd appreciate taking a few minutes or a day to thoughtfully process and ensure that your best self is responding.

Especially in high-trust relationships, you could also consider asking for a redo. Just say, "I don't think the way I said that worked very well. As I've thought more about it, I realize I should have made a few adjustments. Would it be OK if I rewound the clock and tried that again the way I think I should have done it the first time?" People will often be incredibly appreciative and gracious, because they too would benefit from redos.

All these strategies are designed to keep you and others open and curious rather than defensive in the midst of tension so that you can ultimately persuade others to do the hard work of change and commitment.

As we saw in part 2, questions have the greatest impact on influence. As a wise mentor of mine once said, "Defensiveness is the weakest posture in a relationship. Curiosity is the strongest."

What else have you found to be helpful for remaining nonanxious and curious amidst tension?

CHAPTER FOURTEEN

Persuade through Pushback

Anxiety can come from an argument or disagreement related to what you're trying to influence. This, as I've said, causes people to fight, flight, or freeze out of self-protection.

I'm reminded of a time when I facilitated a strategic planning session for an executive team. To help them contemplate changes, I asked them to discuss weaknesses and threats to the organization. The CEO hadn't been in the room when I began this part of the discussion, and when he returned to the room, it was apparent from his body language that he didn't approve of the direction I was taking.

As the discussion continued, I subtly leaned over to him and asked how he was feeling about this part of the discussion, to which he whispered strongly back to me: "What are we doing? This is very negative and doesn't seem productive at all!"

I responded: "*The good news* is that we're getting this out in the open. *While it's true that* it's negative, *let me also say* that in a moment we're going to summarize the key items to be addressed and move to a more productive phase."

Just about every natural instinct I had in that moment was to flee or freeze when the CEO confronted me with his harsh disapproval. Instead, I was able to calm my anxiety, and his, by following a framework for persuading when you're put on the spot or taken aback.

This type of formula is often utilized by leaders who regularly respond to crisis and tragedy, like hospital administrators, school superintendents, politicians, and police chiefs. It's designed to discuss hard truths in a calm way while remaining optimistic, which is very important if you want to ultimately persuade others to change or commit.

Recently a product manager that I was coaching said they find this approach to be particularly useful when they are:
- Questioned about decisions and priorities
- Criticized for quality, cost, or timing issues
- Blamed by someone publicly in a meeting
- Put on the spot with a hard question

In another example, a production support team had been getting blamed and attacked for system performance issues. One senior leader called them out in a meeting by saying, "How do you expect us to keep customers if we're having these system performance issues every week?"

One of the production support leaders responded:

"*The good news* here is that we're very aware of the issues and have immediate visibility into them when they arise. *While it's true that* it's an ongoing concern that has yet to be fully resolved, *let me also say* that we have contracted with a well-regarded third party who is able to quickly diagnose and recommend remediation activities. We expect this will be resolved by the end of next week."

Notice the framework follows this pattern:

Positive: something good and reassuring to reduce negativity and increase empathy

Truth: a direct acknowledgment of the issue and its impact

Positive: a forward-looking or optimistic sentiment that could be in the form of a solution to be implemented, a commitment to resolve, or an invitation to collaboration

If tension arises to a point where people in an influence interaction are starting to fight, flight, or freeze, it's essential that you do what you can to diffuse it.

Positive > truth > positive (PTP) can be the key.

In the two examples I've provided, I've used the same scripted language to start each of the three elements:

- *The good news is . . .*
- *While it's true that . . .*
- *Let me also say . . .*

Do you remember the last time you were put on the spot in an aggressive way? It's really hard to remain composed. When tension is high, it can be especially difficult to keep from fighting, flighting, or freezing. Your head may go cloudy, and it could be hard to think of what to say.

That's why it might be useful to have these communication framework prompts memorized.

That said, you'll want to customize this framework with your own language that fits the situation, just like with the other communication patterns we've reviewed.

Work through Objections and Differences

Sometimes persuasion can be difficult because opinions differ. Two people look at more or less the same set of facts and arrive at different conclusions or have different values. When this happens, the fight, flight, or freeze response is often more subtle and nuanced than in a tense confrontation.

In various cultures, pushback can be expressed directly or indirectly. Whether you're dealing a with more subtle or avoidant resistance or directly oppositional stakeholders, the temptation might be to power up, shut down, or freeze.

Powering up doesn't necessarily mean being aggressive; it just means that you're leveraging what power you do have to push them toward your way of thinking. This power might include your subject-matter expertise, an ultimatum, invoking a company policy, monopolizing dialogue, or just using your powers of argument. As we've said, typically these forms of pushing only push people away and should be used only when necessary. They don't generally build leadership influence.

Shutting down is avoidance or giving in too quickly. It might mean getting quiet, going off video, multitasking, or resigning yourself to the situation. Like with powering up, sometimes you may feel shutting down is the best (or safest) approach, though it rarely builds leadership influence.

Note: shutting down is not the same as taking a break or purposely deciding to remain silent on an issue. Sometime silence speaks louder than words. It can be one of the most powerful forms of communication, because it can allow others to arrive at the right conclusion and demonstrates the virtue of meekness, which is not weakness. Meekness is constrained power or power under control.

Shutting down is different. Shutting down is an abdication of power and an avoidance of influence.

Freezing happens when you don't have the mental, emotional, or physical capacity to do anything. Usually this happens when you find yourself in deeper waters than you know how to navigate or are surprised at the events transpiring.

In any of these cases—fight, flight, or freeze—your influence is limited.

To optimize your powers of persuasion in the face of pushback, seek empathetic alignment.

Empathetic alignment means working toward appreciating the other person's perspective and lining up with points of agreement. Typically, it does *not* mean that you agree or disagree with the objection or differences in opinion. Empathetic alignment remains neutral while affirming the value of everyone's perspective.

If you don't remain neutral, you can too quickly cause others to solidify and/or defend their competing position.

Try this four-step communication framework to build empathetic alignment:

1. **Cushion the pushback, concern, or disagreement.** Cushions soften the impact of force. A verbal cushion softens the impact of arguing or disagreeing. It softens the tension by communicating to the other person that you hear their concern and acknowledge the importance of that concern without agreeing or disagreeing with their concern.

If people don't think they are being listened to or valued, they will have their guard up, and it will be hard to persuade them to change their mind. Therefore affirm the other person with a statement like, "Your concern about cost is an important consideration."

Other more generic (and therefore slightly less effective) forms of a cushion are "I can appreciate that," and "I hear you."

2. **Clarify the pushback, concern, or disagreement.** Social scientists, economists, and psychologists have affirmed the frequency and number of cognitive biases and mental shortcuts that humans take when trying to understand another person or situation. If someone has a concern about cost, is it because they had an expected amount in their mind? Is it because they are targeting to stay under a specific budget? Is it because they don't see the value outweighing the investment? We can't just assume. You have to ask.

Additionally, when you ask someone to clarify their concern, you give both of you more time to think about the concern rather than reactively jumping to an argument or decision.

3. **Confirm that the issue they raise is really the issue.** Years ago, a CEO peer group facilitator invited me to join the group he led. (Peer groups typically meet on a regular basis to network, learn, and process big decisions with other executives.) The amount of money and time this facilitator asked for was substantial, so I hesitated to commit. To address my hesitation, he invited me to observe one of the group's meetings. What I saw only solidified my hesitation: I didn't like how he facilitated the meeting. The discussion didn't seem to be that valuable.

After the meeting, I joined the facilitator for lunch, and he asked me what I thought. There were two reasons I didn't want to join the group: (1) it was a big commitment of time and finances, and (2) I didn't think he was a good facilitator. Which reason do you think I gave for not joining? I gave him reason number one. Not only is it less potentially hurtful, it's also less debatable. If I had chosen the other response, he could have argued that he was having an off day, promise he'd change, bring in testimonials from satisfied members, and so on, but it's very difficult to debate that someone does not have enough time or money.

When he heard reason number one, he did what I'm suggesting you *don't* do: he chose to debate my hesitation with me. He didn't argue that I *had* the time and money but that I *would have* the time and money once I started benefiting from his group!

It only pushed me further away, because he wasn't speaking to the real issue.

Many times, perhaps more often than not, the issue or concern someone raises is not the real issue. They say it's time, money, policy, or lack of approvals, but actually it's something they feel less comfortable sharing. Or maybe they don't even realize that something deeper is causing them to hesitate.

Getting someone to talk about the *real* issue requires vulnerability-based trust, but yields much better and lasting results. Try asking a question like:

- *What else besides that causes you to hesitate on this?*
- *Besides that issue, what other concerns do you have?*
- *If that weren't part of this decision, would anything else cause you to be unsure?*

4. Finally, respond to the pushback, concern, or disagreement. I say "finally" because most people want to deal with the issue right away and respond first, before building empathetic alignment or asking clarifying and confirming questions. That's what the peer group facilitator did and what you and I have probably done hundreds of times: hear an issue, knock it down. When you do respond, follow PCE + check-in. Make a point that addresses the concern, connect this point to something that matters to your stakeholders, support it with evidence, and check in for a reaction. If needed, rinse and repeat.

This is the point in the influence process where you're most tempted to overtalk, because anxiety may be higher and you sense you're getting closer to the finish line. PCE + check-in can be incredibly helpful when responding to concerns because it makes your response clear and concise.

With persuasion, slow is fast and fast is slow. PCE will slow you down to the speed of influence.

With the PCE response, you may decide to diminish the concern with a counterpoint. You might admit the concern but try to move the other person past it, or you could try to flip the concern on its head by pointing out that the concern is the reason. As author Ryan Holiday and others have explained, sometimes the obstacle is the way. For instance, if someone hesitates on a time commitment, you might say, "(P) The time required here is *exactly* why you'd want to take this approach. (C) You've mentioned that quality is a top priority for you, so you don't want to cut corners on this effort. (E) For example, you can see on this spreadsheet that we've correlated hours per project with number of errors and have found that errors rates are inversely correlated to time investment. (Check-in) How would you feel about that?"

Ultimately, this CCCR framework (cushion > clarify > confirm > respond) is designed to build empathetic alignment leading to persuasion to change or commit. Notice that the check-in example above moves closer to a positive decision. That's the goal. Keep building vulnerability-based trust, continue to elevate the dialogue, and remain curious.

The themes we've covered from chapter 1 through 14 all repeat themselves as you move closer and closer to gaining buy-in.

CHAPTER FIFTEEN

Consider Whom You're Trying to Change

In the movie *The Pursuit of Happyness*, based on the true story as told in his autobiography, Chris Gardner needs to influence in order to survive. He struggles to sell bone density scanners to doctors to pay his rent and care for his five-year-old son, which leads to homelessness and heartbreak. His persistent visits to physician prospects aren't leading to sufficient results. One day, he realizes that two things will need to change for him to have the influence and security in life he desires.

First, Chris needs to work on himself. He needs to learn to influence with a different message. He aligns his talents in math and numbers, along with his giftedness with people, to influence others to make better investment decisions.

Beyond that, he reaffirms his courage and resolve to rise above his challenges rather than being victimized by them.

Too often we resign or forfeit our influence because we blame and avoid responsibility. Great influence begins not by waiting for people and circumstances to change, but by changing ourselves.

Again, as Bono says, "If you want to change the world, start by changing the world inside you."

Not Everyone Will Change

This is not only true about you and me, it's true about the people we're trying to influence. Many of the people you and I are trying to influence have resigned themselves to the status quo and may be avoiding personal responsibility to change.

I worked with a marriage and family therapist years ago who, after decades of practice, had accepted the fact some people simply will not confront themselves to make needed changes. Many people, at least in parts of their lives, live on the fixed-mindset end of the performance improvement continuum.

Therefore, it's important to weigh how much effort it's worth investing in to get someone to change.

In his classic book *The New Financial Advisor*, Nick Murray suggests that many (especially newer) financial advisors face the problem of having agreed to work with too many clients that are not a good fit for their practice. He uses the traditional story of the Flood as an analogy: Noah only had capacity for two of every species on the ark. As a result, he was carefully selective about whom to let on.

Likewise, financial advisors only have a set amount of capacity in their practice and need to think about the desired characteristics of who gets on. Do we have chemistry? Does this person listen to my perspectives and apply what we've discussed? Do they have capacity to invest a minimum amount of wealth for me to meet my own objectives?

Whether you're a financial advisor or in supply chain operations, you have similar questions to consider.

It's true: sometimes you have no choice of whom you must influence to meet your goals. Many times, though, we can decide to focus our attention on others who contribute to the decisions. For instance, maybe you could move up or down the org chart in seniority. Perhaps there are other influencers across the organization that sway the thinking of others. It's possible you could cut bait on your fishing in one department or division and move to another spot altogether to get the buy-in you desire.

Consider the acronym CAPO to analyze which stakeholders you could focus on:

Chemistry. How well do we connect personally and align in values?

Access. How often does this person show up and open up? Are they guarded or overly busy—or are they available to me?

Potential. How strong do I see this relationship or opportunity becoming with this stakeholder?

Outcomes. What positive results have been or are being shown that would resonate and build momentum with this stakeholder?

If the answers to these questions are generally "strong," "well," or "frequent," it's likely that you'll be in tune with this stakeholder. Otherwise, you may want to consider shifting your attention elsewhere if you can.

Musicians know that a capo raises the pitch of a fretted instrument to achieve the desired key. Similarly, you can use CAPO to get in tune with the best stakeholders to move your plans ahead.

Mobilizers versus Talkers

As the author of the best-selling book *The Challenger Sale*, Matt Dixon has discovered important factors that make a stakeholder worth trying to lead and influence. His research has uncovered the seven most common types of stakeholders that you might be trying to influence, regardless of title. They are:

Go-getter. Runs after opportunities and is highly focused on organizational improvement.

Skeptic. Doubts most things and asks lots of questions.

Friend. Encourages and helps you in your efforts to lead and influence.

Teacher. Loves to share insights and ideas with others.

Guide. Provides confidential or insider information to help move a decision along.

Climber. Focuses on their own personal gain and ambition.

Blocker. Avoids change and defends the status quo.

According to Dixon's research, top leaders and influencers spend more of their time pursuing Go-Getters, Teachers, and Skeptics, who are between 0.66 and 1.0 times more likely to drive action relative to the average. He refers to these three stakeholder types as Mobilizers, as compared to the Talkers, who tend to be pursued by mid- to low-performing influencers. The Talkers are the Guides, Friends, and Climbers, and they range from 0.22 to 0.23 times more likely to get decisions made and action to happen.

You can guess why some people avoid the Go-Getters, Teachers, and Skeptics. They might be abrasive, arrogant, or intimidating at times, whereas Guides and Friends will make you feel good. Climbers will sometimes be quick to jump on forward moving trains, but will not help you influence others, since not many people trust a Climber.

Furthermore, according to the research, 38 percent of potential stakeholders are Blockers—to be generally avoided—36 percent are Mobilizers, and 26 percent are Talkers, regardless of their title or level of authority. In other words, you'll find CEOs that are Talkers and supervisors on the shop floor that are Mobilizers.

Your job is to spend more time trying to find and influence the Mobilizers.

Let's go back to Chris Gardner in *The Pursuit of Happyness*.

His first change was to change himself: his offering, attitude and what he was communicating.

The second change Gardner realized he needed to make was whom he was trying to talk to. His pursuit of happiness had to travel through the pursuit of people that he could and would mobilize. One of those people was the resource head for Dean Witter, who would have major influence on whether his internship application would be considered. In a famous scene in the movie, Chris runs into him on the street and gets in his taxi to make his case for an internship (while solving the resource head's Rubik's Cube).

Later, after being hired by the resource head, who was willing to mobilize support on his behalf, Chris misses an appointment with an executive that he'd cold-called for reasons beyond his control and goes all the way to the man's house with his son to apologize. Fortunately, that man, Walter Ribbon, invites Chris and his son to share his skybox at a 49ers game. This executive is not only kind and receptive but introduces Chris to high-capacity colleagues and friends at the game, who later become Chris's clients. Walter Ribbon was a mobilizer with CAPO qualities.

Whom could you be spending more time pursuing in order to have more influence—even if they are a bit intimidating?

Personality and Cultural Preferences

One other factor to consider in whom you're pursuing and how you're pursuing them is their personality.

At some point, you've probably done a personality inventory like the Myers-Briggs Type Indicator (MBTI), the Enneagram, CliftonStrengths, DiSC (Dominance, Influence, Steadiness, and Conscientiousness), or the Hogan Personality inventory. Each of these varies in length, method, and predictive efficacy, but all essentially have a similar message: everyone thinks, communicates, and relates to others in different ways, especially in high-stakes or stressful situations. If you want to maximize trust, leadership, and influence, it's important to consider preferred styles of interacting and communicating.

For example, if someone is a high D in the DiSC assessment, it means they are a Driver, who wants to cut to the chase, with low patience for details. If you tend to be a high C, making you more cautious, reflective, and interested in the details, you might want to prepare yourself for some tension. To mitigate that tension, do your best to keep to the big picture as much as possible, go into details only as needed or requested, and be ready to move more quickly than you might normally.

The same can be said for cultural differences. Some cultures value more personal connection before moving to conversations about work. Other cultures prefer spending extra time to analyze a decision before making it. Still other cultures have a more "act, then analyze" approach.

Try to consider the tendencies of others so that you can flex your style to meet them where they are.

Does this mean that you should put everybody into a stereotypical box of assumptions about how they will act and respond? No, of course not. These preferences are somewhat fluid, and everyone is different.

Does it mean that you should act like a chameleon and change the way you communicate with everyone based on their personality and cultural preferences? Well, it depends. If you *can* change to meet them where they are at, you're doing an act of service. If you're *anxiously* changing your preferences and styles because you're willing to be anyone to anybody, you're losing yourself in the process.

Just consider the kind of person that you're trying to influence and what adjustments might make sense to maximize trust and impact.

What If You Don't See Things the Same Way?

In a meeting among leading United States civil rights leaders shortly after Robert F. Kennedy was appointed attorney general in 1961, Martin Luther King Jr. apparently slammed his hand on the table and asked, "Does anyone here have anything positive to say about our new attorney general?"

"No," came the consensus opinion.

"I'm releasing you into the world to find one positive thing to say about Bobby Kennedy, because that one positive thing will be the door through which our movement will have to pass," responded Dr. King.

Through a shared friendship with Kennedy's bishop, these leaders came to appreciate him and converted him to the cause of civil rights. They found the door.

Bono, the lead singer of U2, who wrote songs about Dr. King, explains that his own methodology of influence (and he has influenced foreign and economic policy across the world) centers on this idea: find a door you can both walk through. Too often we overfocus on differences in views rather than finding something important that all parties can agree on.

However different your stakeholders might be, however much you dislike or disagree with them, try to find a door you can walk through.

Influence is about building trust and collaborative decision-making and helping stakeholders to be less guarded or prescriptive. Some will never get there, but many will if you keep trying.

The Final Push

Clara considered her options for a split second after Leon had essentially shut her down.

She'd had several realizations in her influence course about how and whom she tries to persuade.

For one, she'd become more aware of how reactively she goes into problem-solving mode when there's some disagreement or tension. She hadn't thought of this as a by-product of anxiety, since she'd thought of anxiety as worry, but she was expanding her definition and awareness of anxiety. She realized that discomfort with challenging people dynamics caused her impulsively to try to make the anxiety go away. She was a good problem solver, so naturally she'd use this skill to resolve tension.

The other epiphany for Clara came in the analysis of *whom* she should be putting extra effort into. Was Leon a Mobilizer or a Talker? Would he ultimately waste her time, remaining risk-averse, or would he really advocate for her efforts if she won him over? He was hard to work with, but he seemed to be a Go-Getter and a Skeptic. She remembered how he'd asked her challenging questions when she presented this idea.

As these thoughts raced through her mind, she took a breath to get past the fight-or-flight reaction after he'd given her the push-back.

"Leon, timing and capacity are important considerations. Can you tell me more about how the marketing campaigns and pricing increase conflict with the ability to participate in this event?"

"Well, it's a team bandwidth thing really. I realize it's not too much for our customers. It's about what our marketing team can handle."

"That's important to consider. So if your team felt like they could handle the effort on this, you'd support it? It's really just about the team's ability to handle it?"

"Yes, if Emma felt they could do it. They are down one person, and Emma has a lot going on."

"I'd love to talk with Emma briefly about this. It's possible she might view our team's involvement as an addition to her efforts to drive client retention rather than something that will deplete her team's work. I think we're talking about two weeks of attention to this by her and the team, and we're going to do 99 percent of the work for her. Do you think we could arrange for me to talk with her?"

"I'm not sure, Clara. I'll send her a quick email and copy you on it, suggesting a fifteen-minute call, but I want to protect her time."

"Thank you for trusting me to appropriately press a bit."

Clara hung up and texted John: "Well, that worked! His head of marketing is resisting this but agreed to let me talk with her."

"Great!" he replied. "Put those influence skills to work! Would it be helpful to practice or discuss how you'll approach her?"

"That will take time and out of my comfort zone, but that's probably why we should do it! Now good?"

PART FIVE

Institutionalizing Leadership Influence

CHAPTER SIXTEEN

Coaching for Improved Performance

Many teams and organizations that work to improve influence tell me that people around them don't reinforce their efforts. On the contrary, they reinforce taking orders and responding to requests.

One technology leader told me that she was pulled aside by her counterpart in product management who said, "Jen, I hear you are putting your team through a training program to help them influence."

"Yes."

"Well," the product leader continued, "I don't think that's such a good idea. Our team is much closer to the customer, and we know what they want. I'm afraid our teams will be arguing all the time about where to focus our efforts. Our team should dictate that, and your team should build to our requirements."

Fortunately, Jen had the confidence and willingness to influence her counterpart to embrace a new paradigm where technology and product worked together as relatively equal partners. Jen also has worked diligently to coach and reinforce influence for her department despite their discomfort and resistance.

The ultimate proof to the skeptics will be the value that each person is able to bring through their attempts at influence.

Improving How You and Your Team Think and Talk

My friend John, who runs a technology company, often says, "The goal of a leader should be to level the playing field, not make the plays." Leaders can do that by fostering an environment that's conducive to leadership influence and helping people improve their ability to act as influencers.

If you were coaching an actor before a performance, you'd have them rehearse their lines.

If you were coaching an athlete before a competition, you'd have them practice and train.

As a leader, mentor, friend, or parent, you also have opportunities to help others improve key skills.

Every Leader Is a Coach

After nearly twenty years of helping people improve key skills at work, I've come to realize that absolutely nothing beats ongoing coaching.

Coaching can be planned or spontaneous, and it can be done before or after the times when the skill to be coached is needed most.

Whenever it happens, here are the four steps for the most effective skill coaching. If you're the one *needing* the coaching, consider sharing these four steps with those who will be coaching you.

1. **Get buy-in.** Help the person who is being coached acknowledge that they need to and want to improve, and that they can and will get better at the skill in a particular situation or with similar stakeholders.

You could say something here like, "Thanks for letting me join that meeting. Would it be OK if I offered an idea for how you might adjust how you communicated during one part of that meeting?"

Or you could get their buy-in by asking a thought-provoking question like, "What benefit would there be to you if you could get other people talking more in your meetings?"

2. **Explain or show what you expect.** One step that many coaches overlook, especially in communication-related coaching, is the need for them to show and tell. In other words, they assume the person being coached knows and understands things that they really don't fully know or understand (or have forgotten).

Ted Williams was one of baseball's greatest hitters. But he couldn't coach. He was extremely talented, but he couldn't properly explain to others what they needed to know and do. Great coaches make their instructions clear, simple, and memorable. Plus, when possible, they *show* what they explain—through video, illustration, story, or demonstration.

3. **Have them practice until you're satisfied.** This is the most awkward but most important step in the skill coaching process, and it's central to psychologist Anders Ericsson's deliberate practice model. You'll need to ask the other person to practice (demonstrate) what they ideally will (or should have) said or done during a given situation.

You're likely to feel that having the coachee practice it once is enough. No one wants to inflict pain on someone else by asking them to do it again. But until they have done it to your satisfaction, that's exactly what needs to happen so that they feel successful. It's not enough to have them practice once, give some feedback, and say, "OK, so you got it now? Great!"

Even so, pick your battles so you win the war. You might see three changes the person you're coaching needs to make, but you also know that, when it comes to the situations they need to be prepared for, only two of the three changes matter a lot. You also anticipate that their energy and attention will wane by the third piece of coaching. In that case, stick with two, or with whatever number you think is profitable coaching.

4. **Give encouragement.** Ultimately people need the confidence and motivation to put their skill into action. Consider saying something like, "You nailed that introduction. I especially liked how specific and relevant your story was. If you keep using specific, relevant evidence like that, you'll build enormous credibility, which I know is important to you."

Notice what's going on in that statement above. The encouragement referenced something that the coachee did or said. It then made a forward-looking statement such as, "If you continue to do this in the future, you will . . ." Finally, the encouragement mentioned something important to the person being coached. This, of course, only works if the coach has heard what the person being coached really values. Assuming you have, it's demonstrating influence by making the motivation intrinsic to the other person. It's *their* reason for improving.

Let's take the difficult road of skill coaching. If we do, we'll land in beautiful destinations filled with greater trust, culture and impact.

That's influence.

CHAPTER SEVENTEEN

Reinforcing Thought and Communication Patterns

Dale Carnegie facilitators have been coaching people to improve their relationships and communication for decades. Over that time, one of the most important discoveries about helping people grow has been that performance change requires a skill set and a mindset change. Skill set change is defined as anything you do, and mindset change as anything you think and feel about yourself and others.

In other words, you're not going to get better results influencing unless you keep trying better patterns for communicating with others and thinking about those opportunities.

To improve both the skill set and the mindset, I've found the following ongoing practices to be essential:

Reading. Books, articles, and audiobooks can be great resources to better understand the psychology and practice of influence. Historical works like *Team of Rivals: The Political Genius of Abraham Lincoln* by Doris Kearns Goodwin provide compelling examples of great influence that led to sustainable trust and change. Every book about leadership and influence adds to your repertoire of tools and examples. You can also follow me at www.mattnorman .com, where I write regular articles on related topics and maintain a list of resources. I highly recommend studying a book or other resource with a small group, where you can discuss topics and progress.

Podcasts. At the time of this publication, I'm listening to At the Table, with Patrick Lencioni; the Andy Stanley Leadership Podcast; Take Command, a Dale Carnegie podcast; and the Knowledge Project.

Training and coaching programs. I'm biased toward Dale Carnegie action-learning cohort programs, where you can learn from others, practice with others, and make commitments to others. Many other programs, instructor-led and on-demand, as well as private coaching arrangements, can be excellent ways to learn and improve your skill set and mindset. Anyone serious about being an excellent leader and influencer should probably take at least one course per year or work with a coach for at least three months per year. In fact, Dale Carnegie offers a cohort-style program that I built to help people learn and apply the concepts in this book.

It *can* be beneficial to attend a conference, though conferences often immerse attendees in lots of content over a short period of time with little sleep. The important thing here is taking great notes, reviewing those notes, doing something with them, and not trying to do everything possible right away.

Reference resources. Whether it's a poster on the wall or a reminder app on people's phones, reminding people of the influence patterns will drive ongoing application. Consider which reminders and reinforcements best work for you and your team, and utilize them for the most important practices you want to remember.

As Peter Brown and the other authors of *Make It Stick: The Science of Successful Learning* explain, learning loss is inevitable, but don't get cynical about your ability to retain and grow. Keep forcing yourself to recall learnings that are no longer in your short-term memory; as you do, they will solidify in your long-term memory. There are no shortcuts to learning, they write: you just need to keep facing the regular discomfort of consuming ideas, making sense of them, remembering them, and applying them.

What could you do to further reinforce gains in influence?

CHAPTER EIGHTEEN

The Culture of Influence

Behaviors and thoughts reinforced over time become your identity at an individual level and your culture at a group level.

If you want to *be* a person of influence and *have* a culture of influence, you'll need to cast votes for it every day. Every day, you'll need to say "yes" and "well done" and "this is what good looks like."

Identity and culture guide the choices you make, and actions become your identity and culture.

People need to see themselves as having earned a seat at the table and having the credibility to go upstream, where decisions are made.

At a group or organizational level, you might consider taking some of the following actions on a regular basis to form culture and identity around influence:

Write down your values and competencies. Most professional organizations and teams have some documentation of their values and desired competencies for people on that team or organization.

Perhaps when a team is small, values and desired competencies are implied and understood through stories and modeling. But as an organization grows, it's helpful to write down what matters and what shared commitments people will have.

Several years ago, a large company in the central United States realized that their influence suffered because most employees avoided difficult conversations. (I note their location because in that part of the country, people pride themselves on being "Midwest nice," which can result in conflict avoidance.)

This company declared that "Productive Discourse" would be one of their core values, with related leadership competencies to nudge and describe the type of conversations they believed their people *needed* to be having. As a result of this declaration, thousands of employees across the world regularly contemplate how their choices and behaviors reflect a spirit of Productive Discourse.

Integrate values into hiring and performance management. At the aforementioned company, Productive Discourse goes beyond just a lofty aim. It informs whom and how they hire, coach, and review team members.

Interview questions have been designed to flush out the degree to which candidates demonstrate Productive Discourse. Employee training has been built to help people develop it. And leaders coach and review team members on how well and frequently they demonstrate it. This leads to compensation adjustments and promotions.

If you want to advance an influence agenda, incorporate the values and competencies into your talent management practices.

Celebrate wins. People tend to do what's celebrated. It's the human instinct: to do what pleases the crowd, because it feels great to be affirmed. Therefore, if you want people to utilize the skill set and mindset presented in this book, celebrate it when you see it.

You can do this privately or publicly. You can do it in meetings, spontaneously, or in writing. You can do it over email, in a newsletter, or on your website. The key is to see it and celebrate it.

Find ways to measure progress. I've found several metric categories to be particularly useful for measuring progress.

One category is reaction to efforts you're making to coach, develop, and reward influence ability. After an intervention or initiative, you could survey people to see how they felt about that initiative and how helpful they perceived it to be. You can also do a survey like this on a regular basis to keep a pulse on how people feel about the support they are getting.

Before and after behavior frequency can be another helpful measurement. Use this book to create a list of behaviors that reflect influence and work in your environment. Then have people assess how frequently they and/or others demonstrate that specific behavior on a scale. Ideally this is measured both before and after a training program, coaching, or other effort to help them improve.

Finally, you might consider estimating the organizational impact of this skill set and mindset by asking people to estimate its dollar value, either in hard, direct, bottom-line terms or in terms of soft gains such as in productivity and efficiency. You might also track relevant key performance indicators (KPI) for your organization. Viewing a trend line or comparing the KPI of one group to a control group that hasn't worked on influence can reveal the ROI of these efforts.

Measuring progress may be time-consuming, but it can be extremely important for building the case for change and showing people the difference they are making.

Give awards. As we've said, people like to be appreciated. An award makes an ongoing public declaration of the behaviors that matter.

I'll never forget the privilege I once had to join the Hy-Vee supermarkets' annual Service Awards ceremony. Each of the recipients for the year is profiled with specific stories of their exceptional service to customers. The company executive team is on hand to present awards, press releases are issued for each individual recipient, and the photos of recipients are displayed on the sides of Hy-Vee distribution trucks. It sends a loud message to the entire company: exceptional service matters a lot.

Now you may or may not think that influence matters a lot. If you believe it's just nice to have, I wouldn't recommend going crazy on awards. But if you do think it's central to the success of your team or organization's future, you might be ready for some awards.

Conduct regular organizational assessments. We've mentioned assessments already. Doing an employee engagement or climate survey can often indicate organizational health and the impact of your leaders. If leaders and teams are working transactionally, treating one another like functionaries and order takers, it's unlikely that the team will score high on an engagement survey. The converse is true as well. Regular surveys (probably once every year or every other year) can provide great insights on team member perspectives.

A closing thought about rewards and recognition: don't worry about making it perfect, as that can be the enemy of "good enough." Just start with one form of reinforcement and follow through consistently. Small actions over time can drive the greatest gains.

Prepping for Success

John called Clara and began by trying to build additional psychological safety for her to relax and practice with him.

"Thanks for your willingness to talk this through, Clara. It's a bit vulnerable to game plan and practice when you're an accomplished professional, but I always find it makes a difference. Would it be helpful for me to give a quick perspective on how to approach this?"

"Yes, that's great!"

"OK. I think I'd position this up front with Emma as an opportunity for her to further expand and elevate the value of marketing across Agrifoods, ultimately aligning her to community and environmental impact. I might reply to her off Leon's email with something like:

> Emma, it sounds like you're working on multiple strategic efforts next quarter.
>
> Why don't we find just fifteen minutes to talk about whether we could partner to expand and elevate your team's value even further through an Agrifood community engagement effort.
>
> For example, John MacLennan has personally told me how excited he is for Bioengineering to be taking a lead role in this important project.
>
> Maybe your team would benefit from the added visibility and alignment to broader enterprise priorities.
>
> Could we discuss how it might connect to your goals and how we could minimize the work needed from your team?

"That's just my take, Clara. I don't know if you want to mention my name, but I'm fine if you do."

"Yes, I love that approach."

John wanted to leave it at that, assuming Clara got it. He didn't want to make her feel like a rookie. She'd been in plenty of high-level, high-stakes meetings. Nonetheless, he knew the value of deliberate practice, so he asked, "What would be your version of that?"

"My version would be close to that. I think I'd write:

Emma, Leon mentioned that you have a few important campaigns and a price increase happening right now, so I'll be quick.

I'm working with other senior Agrifood leaders to drive customer retention while advancing a key enterprise-wide community engagement opportunity.

For instance, John MacLennan has personally been focused on this effort and has commented how much he hopes Bioengineering will take a lead role.

Perhaps I could facilitate this without hardly any effort of your part during your busy quarter.

Would you be open to a brief conversation about how this might align with your goals?

"Clara, I love how empathetic and direct that is. That tone will likely position a productive discussion with Emma."

Emma did respond favorably to the meeting request. She and Clara had a surprisingly great call. Clara had anticipated more resistance but got very little. Maybe she caught Emma on a better day than Leon had, or maybe Clara's approach lessened Emma's pushback.

Clara opened the call with Emma asking a few open-ended questions in a relaxed tone, not trying to push any agenda. She intentionally made sure her questions were bigger-picture, such as, "What vision do you have for your team?" and "What are some wins you'd like to personally help support in the next year?"

Clara was very thoughtful in her listening and empathizing with Emma, both about her goals and her constraints. Emma sincerely felt that Clara was a friend.

Ten minutes into the conversation, Clara made a couple of quick points about suggested next steps for Bioengineering's involvement, and Emma totally supported them.

Clara knew she'd won Emma over when Emma made a point at the end of the call to suggest they grab a glass of wine sometime to talk more.

Emma committed to circling back with Leon to voice her support and ensure they were visible, leading advocates for Clara's work.

It wasn't lost on Clara that she was sitting in the same coffee shop, once again sipping a latte, waiting for John to arrive. This was where it all started.

John swept around the corner into her view with a smile.

"Way to go, champ," he said as he fist-bumped Clara.

"You too, John. The event exceeded everyone's expectations, including my own. I think this effort has great momentum!"

"I couldn't agree more. I'm so excited."

"John, it's not just this effort. Your guidance and my improved mindset and skill set around influence has had a profound impact."

"I'm so glad, Clara."

"John, I have to admit, even though I'm an accomplished leader, I haven't really been a true collaborative influencer. I've gotten to where I am by working hard, making good choices, developing expertise where needed, and just being a nice person. That all has some influence *over* others but it's not really influencing *through* others.

"Even at home, I'm less anxious about doing, doing, doing . . . solving, solving, solving . . . driving, driving, driving. It's hard to explain. Now I'm much more aware of when to slow down, when to let others talk, when to let go of control so that I'm guiding and engaging others, including my kids and husband. Thank you."

"It's a lifelong journey we're on, Clara. Your desire to keep growing makes you an incredible partner and friend."

CHAPTER NINETEEN

Conclusions About Leading With Influence

L et's go back to where we began this book: it's challenging to get the attention and engagement of others in your ideas for change. True, some ideas are so good that people can't avoid paying attention. True, sometimes you have so much trust or authority that people can't avoid listening. It's also true that some people will never listen no matter how hard you try.

But many times people will listen if you approach the interaction in the best way possible. Here are some major points:

- Build psychological safety so people will let their guard down.
- Elevate the dialogue so that people will be inspired and aligned.
- Open the interaction in a way that invites more expansive conversation.
- Ask more and better questions to get others to come to shared conclusions.
- Distill the interests of others into short, memorable phrases to help them build momentum.

- Explain your recommendations in a way that people will hear and respond.
- Respond to hesitation and pushback in a way that builds trust and alignment.
- Coach and reinforce a cultural movement toward trust-based relationship influence.

As we've said, it probably won't be easy. We all have comfort zones, which means there are skills and approaches that feel awkward and intimidating. It's usually more comfortable to stay in your lane, go to others when you need them, and use your expertise to advance your agenda. But that won't optimize trust, innovation, or your engagement with the broader team and its purpose.

If it's easy, it's probably not worth doing. Leading with influence *is* worth doing.

Selected Bibliography

Introduction

Cialdini, Robert. *Influence: The Psychology of Perception*. New York: Harper Business, 2006.

Dweck, Carol. *Mindset: The New Psychology of Success*. New York: Ballantine, 2007.

Ericsson, Anders, and Robert Pool. *Peak: Secrets from the New Science of Expertise*. San Francisco: HarperOne, 2017.

Ma, Yo-Yo. "Case Study: Balancing Structure and Emotion." MasterClass website.

Maxwell, John. *The 21 Irrefutable Laws of Leadership*. Nashville: HarperChristian Resources, 2022. Chapter 1.

Norman, Matt. *Four Patterns of Healthy People*. Minneapolis: Matt Norman, 2020. Chapter 2.

Pink, Daniel. *To Sell Is Human*. New York: Riverhead, 2013. Chapter 1.

Rackham, Neil. *SPIN Selling*. New York: McGraw-Hill, 1988. Chapter 1, Huthwaite corporation study.

Chapter 1: Prioritize Availability over Productivity

Berry, Wendell. *Life is a Miracle*. New York: Counterpoint, 2001.

Christensen, Clayton. *How Will You Measure Your Life?* New York: HarperCollins, 2012.

Edmonson, Amy. *The Fearless Organization*. Hoboken, N.J.: Wiley, 2018.

Hummel, Charles. *Tyranny of the Urgent*. Chicago: IVP, 1994.

Newport, Cal. *A World Without Email*. New York: Portfolio, 2021.

Palmer, Parker. *A Hidden Wholeness*. San Francisco: Jossey-Bass, 2009.

Chapter 2: Build both Predictive and Vulnerability-Based Trust

Brown, Brene. *Atlas of the Heart*. New York: Random House, 2022. Chapter 1.

Coyle, Daniel. *The Culture Code*. New York: Bantam, 2018. Chapter 8.

Lencioni, Patrick. *The Five Dysfunctions of a Team*. San Francisco: Jossey-Bass, 2002.

Nadella, Satya. *Hit Refresh*. New York: Harper Business, 2017.

Project Aristotle. "Project Aristotle: A Case Study in Psychological Safety." LeaderFactor website.

Chapter 3: Pay Attention to the Little Things

Argyris, Chris. *The Fifth Discipline Fieldbook*. New York: Crown Currency, 1994.

Boothman, Nicholas. *How to Make People Like You in 90 Seconds or Less*. New York: Algonquin Young Readers, 2008. Chapter 2.

Carnegie, Dale. *How to Win Friends and Influence People*. New York: Simon & Schuster, 2022.

Lindegaard, Gitte, Gary Fernandes, Cathy Dudek, and Judith M. Brown. "Attention Web Designers: You Have 50 Milliseconds to Make a Good First Impression!" *Behaviour and Information Technology* 25, no. 2 (March 2006): 115–26.

Schmall, Tyler. "This Is Exactly How Long You Have to Make a Good First Impression." *New York Post* website. Updated Feb. 29, 2019.

Wargo, Eric. "How Many Seconds to a First Impression?" Association for Psychological Science website, July 1, 2006.

Chapter 4: Be like a Salmon

Carnegie, Dale. *How to Stop Worrying and Start Living*. New York: Simon & Schuster, 1990.

Chapter 5: Use Value Language

Egnal, Bart. *Leading through Language*. Hoboken, N.J.: Wiley, 2015.

Chapter 6: Talk like a Palace Builder

Barrett, Lisa Feldman. "Your Brain Is Not for Thinking." *New York Times*, Nov. 23, 2020.

Bower, Gordon. "Narrative Stories as Mediators for Serial Learning." *Psychonomic Science* 14 (April 1969): 181–82.

Davis, Alison. "To Improve Your Storytelling Skills, Use Abraham Lincoln as Inspiration." *Inc.*, Feb. 2018.

Graesser, A. L., N. L. Hoffman, and L. F. Clark. "Structural Components of Reading Time." *Journal of Verbal Learning & Verbal Behavior* 19, no. 2 (1980): 135–52.

Lencioni, Patrick. *Death by Meeting*. San Francisco: Jossey-Bass, 2004.

Neimand, Annie. "Science of Story Building: Narrative Transportation." *Medium*, May 2018.

"What Is Employee Engagement and How Do You Improve It?" Gallup Workplace website.

Chapter 7: Explore the Four Parts of Human Thinking That Drive Influence

Buber, Martin. *I and Thou*. Translated by Walter Kaufmann. New York: Scribner's, 1970.

Damasio, Antonio. *Descartes' Error*. New York: Penguin, 2005.

Morse, Gardiner. "Decisions and Desire." *Harvard Business Review*, Jan. 2006.

Chapter 8: Develop the Art of Facilitation

Collins, Jim. *Good to Great*. New York: Harper Business, 2001. Chapter 4.

Dewar, Carolyn, and Scott Keller. "Four Motivation Mistakes Most Leaders Make." *Harvard Business Review*, Oct. 2011.

Dixon, Matthew, and Brent Adamson. *The Challenger Sale*. New York: Portfolio, 2011.

Fritz, Robert. *The Path of Least Resistance*. New York: Ballantine, 1989.

Tik, Martin, et al. "Ultra-high-field fMRI Insights on Insight: Neural Correlates of the Aha! Moment." *Human Brain Mapping*, April 2018: 1–12.

Chapter 9: Summarize Regularly

Welch, Jack. *Winning*. New York: Harper Business, 2005.

Chapter 10: Explain in a Way That Will Resonate

Ebbinghaus, Hermann. *Memory*. Monograph. University of Berlin, 1885.

Chapter 11: It's Not Just What You Say, but How You Say It

Van Zant, Alex, and Jonah Berger. "How the Voice Persuades." *Journal of Personal and Social Psychology* 118, no. 4 (April 2020): 661–82.

Chapter 12: Be a Nonanxious Presence

Friedman, Edwin. *A Failure of Nerve*. New York: Seabury, 2007.

Schnarch, David. "The Crucible 4 Points of Balance." Crucible Institute website, Jan. 2011.

Chapter 13: Respond instead of Reacting

Bono, *Surrender*. New York: Knopf, 2022.

Nestor, James. *Breath: The New Science of a Lost Art*. New York: Riverhead, 2020.

Chapter 14: Persuade through Pushback

Holiday, Ryan. *The Obstacle Is the Way*. New York: Portfolio, 2014.

Chapter 15: Consider Whom You're Trying to Change

Dixon, Matt. "To Get Results That Count, You Better Learn These Seven Customer Profiles." LinkedIn, Sept. 2015.

Murray, Nick. *The New Financial Advisor*. New York: Nicholas Murray, 2001.

Chapter 17: Reinforcing Thought and Communication Patterns

Brown, Peter, Henry Roediger, and Mark McDaniel. *Make It Stick*. Cambridge, Mass.: Harvard University Press, 2014.

Goodwin, Doris Kearns. *Team of Rivals: The Political Genius of Abraham Lincoln*. New York: Simon & Schuster, 2006.

Acknowledgments

Several years ago, an organizational psychologist brought the problem of collaborative influence to my attention. She initially wanted nothing to do with me or my services until she offhandedly threw out this question before hanging up: "Can you help technical people shift from being order takers to business partners?"

That question, her healthy skepticism, and her willingness to tell others about our success in solving this problem has led to thousands of smart people building better relationships and getting their ideas heard. Thank you, Anne, and the dozens of HR leaders and executives who have understood this problem, not just for technologists, and invested in solving it. People see themselves differently, and organizations have made great gains because of it.

A special appreciation to my wife, Kari, who challenges and pushes my thinking every day. You are a true influencer. And to my smart and thoughtful friend John Tedesco, who generously read and provided perspectives (which ultimately led to the story about Clara).

Thank you to my colleagues at Dale Carnegie, who have embraced these concepts and have found opportunities for us to do this important advocacy around influence. To Scotty, Amy, our team across the North Central United States, and to Joe, Christine, Rob, Dan, Ercell, Jean-Louis, and the rest of our global leadership team: I'm honored to be your teammate in the work of helping people and organizations realize their untapped potential.

About the Author

Matt Norman coaches and advises executives on how to build great people and culture. He is president and CEO of Norman & Associates. As the largest North American provider of Dale Carnegie programs, Norman & Associates offers custom coaching and consulting in the areas of talent strategy, personal effectiveness, planning, and goal alignment to help people improve how they communicate, lead, influence, and work together. Matt is regularly recognized as a top revenue producer, executive coach, facilitator, speaker, and leader of award-winning teams. He has been named to the Minnesota Business Power 50 for his contributions to the community. He's also the award-winning author of *Four Patterns of Healthy People: How to Grow Past Your Rooted Behaviors, Discover a Deeper Connection with Others, and Reach Your Full Potential in Life and Business*; *Flourishing Leadership*; and *Flourishing Couples*. You can find his articles on personal and organizational effectiveness at www.mattnorman.com. Matt loves being a husband and father of three, enjoying shared activities like skiing, mountain biking, trail running, and music.

Continue with Dale Carnegie:
Dale Carnegie Training Overview

www.dalecarnegie.com
It's Time to Take Command
Individuals | Teams | Organizations

Apply the proven tools, expertise, and support of Dale Carnegie and watch the effects ripple. From individual breakthroughs to transformed relationships, to radically changed team performance, measurable results, organizational impact, and reshaped cultures.

At Dale Carnegie, we've helped thousands of organizations and millions of individuals take command—of their businesses, their careers, and their futures.

Communications | Sales & Service | Leadership |
Presentations | Activated Organizations

Learn from Anywhere

In Person—Certified instructors facilitate engaging, high-energy, collaborative classes. Over 200 locations globally, offered in over 80 countries and in over 30 languages.

Live Online—Our leading virtual instructor-led training programs bring people together to solve complex challenges, increase productivity, and deliver results. Offered globally in over 30 languages.

All on Dale Carnegie eVolve: Central to the modern blended learning experience is eVolve. The simple, elegant user interface integrates digital, live virtual, and live in-person training into a seamless, blended learning solution. Create and sustain performance change through social collaboration, interactive tools, and support from our world-class trainers.

Whether taking an in-person, live online, or on demand course, access to eVolve enhances the Dale Carnegie experience.

Learn More: www.dalecarnegie.com

The Dale Carnegie Programs and Website

www.dalecarnegie.com

Lead with Influence (The Course)

The knowledge held by leaders with technical or functional expertise is invaluable to organizations. *Lead with Influence* will empower these professionals through a neuroscience-backed, proven process to help gain commitment from others.

Empower yourself with the tools to lead change, overcome resistance, and put your ideas to work for your organization.

Gain a proven process for engaging others in more meaningful conversation about change and new ideas. The process follows these four steps:

1. **Position:** Demonstrate that you're a trusted partner and invite more strategic dialogue.
2. **Probe:** Ask better questions that cause others to engage and think differently.
3. **Propose:** Explain your ideas and recommendations in an engaging way.
4. **Persuade:** Handle pushback, manage anxiety and get commitment.

Superpower your ability to influence others and gain cooperation. Write more effective emails, run meetings that yield activity and outcomes, deliver compelling presentations, and have productive conversations. By making these improvements, you'll deepen trust with others who have competing priorities or perspectives. This will result in stronger results for you and your organization.

Beyond these results, you'll increase engagement in your work as you increase alignment between what you do and the outcomes you're driving.

The Dale Carnegie Course: Effective Communications and Human Relations

Whether you are starting out in your career or have reached a point where you could use a reboot, the methodology of the Dale Carnegie Course can provide you with the mindset and skillset to achieve better and different results. Expand both your personal and professional capabilities and capacity with intentionality. The Dale Carnegie Course and the Effective Communications and Human Relationships course will give you the confidence and competence to gain the command you need in your career and personal life.

1. Build on confidence and personal leadership competence.
2. Strengthen skills in relating to others and build inclusivity in your organization.
3. Enhance skills to communicate logically, clearly, and concisely. Energize and engage listeners. Listen with empathy.
4. Develop leadership skills to take charge of your life, be more flexible and innovative, inspire others, and motivate others to action.
5. Power yourself to control attitudes and reduce stress so you can be at your optimum best.

Dale Carnegie Leadership Courses

Effective leaders recognize their actions that may have both intended and unintended consequences, so they carefully consider the culture that their actions will help shape. They recognize that by creating a positive climate, they inspire teams and influence them to contribute their best.

1. Develop Your Leadership Potential: Stop Doing, Start Leading
2. Leadership Training for Results: Unleash Talent in Others

High-Impact Presentations

Being an outstanding communicator is one of the most important and critical skills a professional can work to achieve. An effective communicator can help sort out the deluge of information the average person is surrounded with and impart it to others to lead, influence, and inspire. The High Impact Presentations course focuses on structuring an effective presentation that builds credibility and engages your audience while clearly and persuasively conveying your message. Participants explore the optimum use of voice and gesture to create a lasting impression—as well as a variety of presentation styles ranging from a formal speech to casual meeting or contentious conversation.

Sales Training

Learn how to build productive relationships built on reciprocal trust that comes from established credibility and a mutual understanding of value. These relationships happen when the seller can demonstrate a genuine comprehension of the client's world—

their real needs—based on asking powerful questions and listening skills that identify opportunities and challenges and uncover unknown or unexpressed requirements. In an environment where the seller can't always win on price, it's important to be focused on the real customer wants and needs that will ensure mutual success. Dale Carnegie's proprietary Sales Model and Process is adaptable within any sales culture and fits any salesperson's style. You should treat sales like you treat other relationships. It's give and take, with a heavy emphasis on give!

1. Winning with Relationship Selling
2. Virtual Selling

For more in-person, live online, and on demand course offerings please visit: www.dalecarnegie.com